CHAMPION

CHAMPION

THE COMEBACK TALE OF THE
AMERICAN CHESTNUT TREE

SALLY M. WALKER

HENRY HOLT AND COMPANY

NEW YORK

Henry Holt and Company, *Publishers since 1866*
Henry Holt® is a registered trademark of Macmillan Publishing Group, LLC
175 Fifth Avenue, New York, NY 10010
mackids.com

CHAMPION: THE COMEBACK TALE OF THE AMERICAN CHESTNUT TREE.
Text copyright © 2018 by Sally M. Walker

Library of Congress Cataloging-in-Publication Data is available.
ISBN 978-1-250-12523-1 (hardcover)
ISBN 978-1-250-12524-8 (ebook)

Our books may be purchased in bulk for promotional, educational, or business use.
Please contact your local bookseller or the Macmillan Corporate and
Premium Sales Department at (800) 221-7945 ext. 5442 or by e-mail at
MacmillanSpecialMarkets@macmillan.com.

First edition, 2018 / Designed by Patrick Collins
Printed in the United States of America by LSC Communications,
Harrisonburg, Virginia.

1 3 5 7 9 10 8 6 4 2

In memory of my father,
DONALD FLEMING MACART,
who always had time for a story

CONTENTS

It takes a noble man to plant a seed
for a tree that will someday give shade
to people he may never meet.

—*attributed to* DAVID ELTON TRUEBLOOD,
American theologian and philanthropist

CHAPTER ONE

DISASTER!

HAVE YOU EVER CLIMBED A TREE? Have you ever breathed in the spicy scent of pine trees or looked closely at a leaf?

Hermann Merkel was a boy who loved being around trees. He loved them so much that when he grew up, caring for trees became his job. Even before the New York Zoological Park hired Merkel in 1898 to be its chief forester, he could identify every tree in the park—and there were *more than a thousand* of them—by the shape of its leaves and the look of its bark. The trees were as familiar to him as the people in his neighborhood. Merkel spent hundreds of hours walking the

When Hermann Merkel first strolled in the garden of the New York Zoological Park, American chestnut trees grew so tall that they seemed to touch the sky.

park's many paths, doing what he liked to do most: looking at trees. The park's 1,500 American chestnut trees were among his favorites. Some of them had trunks so big that Merkel's outstretched arms couldn't completely encircle them. It took two—if not three—people holding hands to do it. Every year on hot summer days, Merkel cooled off in the shade of these trees. Every year after winter frosts arrived, he ate the trees' roasted chestnuts as a sweet, crunchy snack. Every year, that is, until 1904, when disaster struck.

Hermann Merkel was concerned about wounds similar to this one that marred the bark of the park's lovely chestnut trees.

One summer day that year, Merkel found ugly wounds on the trunks of some of his splendid chestnut trees. Their bark had split open and, as with a serious cut in a human's skin, he could see the tissue beneath. When he looked toward the treetops, he saw that the leaves on certain branches had wilted and turned brown. Concerned, Merkel checked other trees: the oaks, the locusts, the birches. All of them looked fine. Only the chestnut trees were hurt. Merkel was unsure what was happening, but it looked like a blight, a disease.

The gargantuan trunks of these American chestnut trees dwarf the men standing beside them.

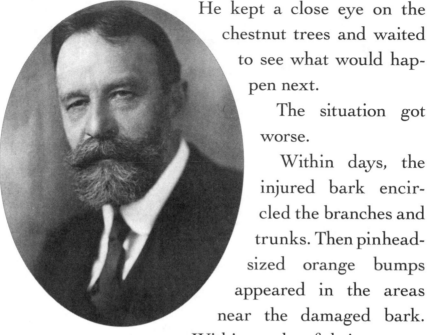

Working as the zoological garden's chief forester was a job that Hermann Merkel enjoyed.

He kept a close eye on the chestnut trees and waited to see what would happen next.

The situation got worse.

Within days, the injured bark encircled the branches and trunks. Then pinhead-sized orange bumps appeared in the areas near the damaged bark. Within weeks of their appearance, all the affected branches died. Merkel didn't know what was attacking his chestnut trees, but he hoped that the approaching winter's cold temperatures would stop it.

Unfortunately, the mysterious blight dashed his hopes the following spring. The disease remained. Even worse, it spread. It killed American chestnut seedlings sprouting in the park's greenhouse. It infected chestnut saplings in the tree nursery outside. It attacked the enormous trunks of hundred-year-old chestnut trees. Determined to save them, Merkel cut off the infected branches. He sprayed the trunks with liquids formulated to kill tree diseases. Nothing halted the blight.

*Workers sprayed the park's chestnut trees, hoping
to kill the disease that was attacking them.*

One after another, the park's magnificent chestnut trees began to die.

Desperate for help, Merkel contacted William Murrill, a scientist at the nearby New York Botanical Garden. Perhaps Murrill would know what was killing Merkel's trees. Maybe he could save them.

THE CULPRIT

Murrill couldn't help until he identified the culprit. The orange bumps that surrounded the ugly wounds gave him an important clue. He thought they looked like the reproductive parts of a fungus. Fungi are organisms that live and grow on organic matter such as plants and animals. This worried Murrill because he knew that some fungi are harmful, even deadly, to other forms of life.

To confirm his suspicions, Murrill collected material from the trees' wounds and put it on a nutritious gel inside a shallow glass container called a petri dish. He covered the dish and waited. Within days, tiny white threads—the sign of a growing fungus—reached across the gel. As days passed, the fungus spread; its color changed from white to yellow. When the fungus was completely grown, it started reproducing. The reproductive parts of the fungus turned a deep orange—the same color as the tiny bumps that Merkel had found on the park's chestnut trees. Murrill had solved the first mystery: A fungus was causing the blight.

Meanwhile, more of the park's chestnut trees were getting sick. But until Murrill figured out how the fungus got inside the trees, he couldn't give Merkel advice on how to stop it. Searching for a way to fight the fungus, Murrill purposely gave the blight to some healthy young chestnut trees in his greenhouse. He smeared a small amount of the blight fungus on their bark. Several weeks passed. Nothing happened.

William Murrill was an expert at identifying plant diseases.

Puzzled, Murrill tried again. This time he scraped a hole in the trees' bark and exposed the tissue beneath. Then he put the fungus directly into the small wounds. Within four to six weeks, all the branches above the wound sites were dead. That solved the second mystery:

Any wound that exposed the tissue layer beneath the bark—a scratch from a squirrel's claw, a hole gouged by a woodpecker, a break caused by the wind snapping off a branch—provided a doorway for the fungus to reach the tree's inner tissue.

Merkel and Murrill were sure the tiny orange bumps they spotted on the bark of American chestnut trees were connected to the disease that was harming the trees.

BENEATH THE BARK

How could a tiny fungus kill a gigantic tree? The answer lies beneath the bark. In a sense, a tree resembles the human body. Its trunk encases the tree's internal tissues in much the same way that the trunk of your body surrounds your heart, liver, and other internal organs. Like your arms, a chestnut tree's branches are extensions off its trunk. Bark, the trunk's outermost covering, is the tree's skin. It protects the tree from pests and diseases and insulates it from extreme weather conditions.

Three layers of tissue lie just under the bark. They control how healthy the tree is and how well it grows. Two of the layers are made of tubular vessels—like super-thin drinking straws. One layer carries nutrients and water from the leaves down to the roots. The other transports nutrients that are absorbed by the tree's roots up to the branches and leaves.

These arrows point to a thin line, which is the cambium. This important layer of cells encircles a tree's trunk and branches and produces the tree's growth cells.

Between the two nutrient transport layers is the third layer, a paper-thin sheet of cells called the cambium. The cambium is very important because it produces the cells that a tree needs to grow. When a large area of the cambium is damaged, it is a severe injury, and death can occur.

Spotting the ugly wounds on a chestnut tree's branches and trunk was easy. But Murrill was unable to solve the third mystery—how the fungus killed the tree—until he looked at the tissue beneath the bark. There he saw that the blight fungus's microscopic threads had fanned out beneath the bark as they sought water and food. The thready network spread throughout the cambium until it encircled the trunk or a branch. Encircling, or girdling, a trunk or branch in this way cuts off the tree's food-supply lines. The parts of the chestnut tree beyond the girdled area starved to death. Appalled, Murrill realized that the fungus was the most destructive kind of parasite—one that killed its host, the plant or animal it grew on. Although he had identified the culprit and discovered how it killed chestnut trees, Murrill was disappointed that he could not find a way to stop it. The only advice he could offer Merkel was to cut down and burn the sickened trees to keep the fungus from spreading.

In 1906, Murrill wrote, "My observations . . . have led me to take a gloomy view regarding the immediate future of the chestnut [tree]. The disease seems destined to run its course . . . and it will hardly be safe to plant young trees while the danger of infection is so great." Throughout the summer he watched as Hermann Merkel lost heart. "I believe he considers the condition quite hopeless. . . . Practically all the chestnut trees within [Merkel's] jurisdiction appear to be dying rapidly. Even the young trees in the nursery [at the zoo] have been either entirely killed or rendered worthless by the fungus."

The dead branches on this tree clearly show which ones have been girdled by the chestnut blight fungus.

By 1911, only two of the 1,500 chestnut trees that had graced the grounds of the New York Zoological Park remained. And foresters, botanists, and chestnut growers in neighboring states reported more alarming news: The blight had spread and was killing the American chestnut trees in their areas, too. Some of them followed Murrill's advice. They cut and burned infected trees. Some experimented with special sprays created to kill fungi. Others resorted to home remedies, such as pouring poison on chestnut tree roots or boring holes into the trunks and filling them with iron nails or sulfur. Nothing worked.

Were American chestnut trees doomed? And why were people so concerned?

CHAPTER TWO

A FOREST GIANT

BEFORE THE BLIGHT STRUCK, American chestnut trees had dominated North America's eastern forests for more than 12,000 years. They towered up to 100 feet tall. Chestnut trees were the forest elders, some living 600 years or even longer. In spring, winds churned their cream-colored catkins into frothy waves at the top of the forest canopy. On their branches during the summer, prickly green burs swelled around the nuts that grew within these envelopes. In autumn, surrounded by a blaze of yellow leaves, the burs split open and rained mahogany-colored nuts on the forest floor.

For thousands of years, American chestnut trees were

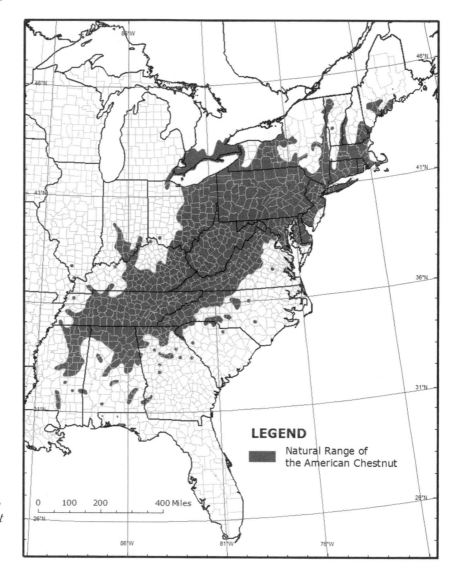

Prior to the blight, American chestnut trees dominated eastern forests.

a combination supermarket, drugstore, and lumberyard for American Indians, who ate the nuts raw, roasted, stewed, and ground into flour.

In the Southeast, the Cherokee boiled the leaves into medicines for heart trouble, stomach complaints, and coughs. They packed chestnut leaves into poultices for sores. Cherokee builders split the wood into shingles for their homes. In the Northeast, the Iroquois treated rheumatism with chestnut leaves and made hair tonic with oil from the nuts. Mothers soothed their babies' chafed skin with chestnut wood ground to a soft powder. Also in the Northeast, Lenape men felled American chestnut trees and crafted the trunks into dugout canoes. Every part of the tree benefited the people who lived nearby.

Spanish explorer Hernando de Soto sought gold when he and his men arrived in North America in 1539. Although they didn't find that precious metal in the Appalachian Mountains, they found plenty of chestnut trees. "Where there be mountaines, there be chestnuts," wrote one of the members of the expedition. In those days, from Maine to Georgia and as far west as Indiana, Kentucky, Tennessee, and parts of Mississippi, one-fourth of the forests' hardwood trees were American chestnut.

European colonists flooded America during the next 200 years. They quickly realized that American chestnut logs, planks, and rails lasted a long time. Tannin, a chemical

American Indians used parts of the chestnut tree in nearly every aspect of their lives.

Even if they had held hands, the Shelton family, who lived in Tennessee, couldn't have completely encircled the trunk of this chestnut tree.

compound found in certain kinds of wood, makes the wood highly resistant to decay. Chestnut wood contains a lot of tannin. In 1792, Thomas Jefferson wrote to George Washington that some of the mountain lands near his home in Virginia had been "inclosed with rail fences, which do not last long (except where they are of chestnut)." Unlike other wood fences, chestnut fences stood firm, often for more than 100 years.

CHESTNUT TREASURE

In January 1876, Pennsylvania farmer Jacob Klinck and his employees were felling a large American chestnut. When the saw was deep inside the tree's six-foot diameter trunk, its teeth suddenly rasped against something harder than wood. Klinck peered into the cut and saw a metallic glint. Worried that it might be an explosive device that had become embedded in the trunk during a Civil War skirmish, Klinck told his men to cut into the trunk from the other side to avoid the metal object.

When the tree finally toppled, gold glittered in the sunlight—a watch and key, two pencil boxes, and a necklace! The watch's cover was inscribed with the date 1740. How had the gold items gotten inside the tree? Klinck could only guess. He knew that a colonial mansion had once stood nearby. Taking into account the age of the watch, Klinck speculated that 100 years earlier, the items had been buried at the base of the tree to hide them from marauders during the Revolutionary War. There they'd been forgotten, and as the years passed, the tree's bark had grown around the objects. Although the hands of the watch had rusted off, its timing mechanism still worked. After having the hands replaced, Klinck happily showed his fancy "new" timepiece to all who were interested.

The wide, straight trunks of chestnut trees were ideal for timber. European settlers quickly realized that the trees were a valuable resource.

Sawyers prized the trees' long, straight trunks that stretched tens of feet skyward before branching. The trunks were not only straight but also enormous. In 1919, a farmer in Quakertown, Pennsylvania, needed 110 pounds of dynamite to blast the stump of a 300-year-old chestnut tree out of the ground. Reportedly, the stump's circumference measured 34 feet, 6 inches. While most chestnut trees did not reach that gargantuan size, many had circumferences of 15 or more feet. Colonists built homes, barns, furniture, and musical instruments from American chestnut wood. They buried their dead in chestnut caskets.

The trees' nuts were treasures of a different sort. Unlike oaks and other nut-bearing trees, the American chestnut reliably produced a crop of nuts every year; they were a valuable food source. How plentiful were the nuts? Very large trees could produce 10 or more bushels, or so people said. But people in rural areas, particularly in Appalachia, also counted on the annual harvest for another reason. Georgia resident Noel Moore recalled seeing whole families—even the children—hauling sacks of chestnuts into the town where he lived in the early 1900s. There, they bartered with shop-keepers for items such as flour, sugar, shoes, and clothes. According to some chestnut growers of the time, a

Many people enjoyed spending time in chestnut groves.

chestnut orchard was "more profitable than many apple orchards."

Before the blight, American chestnut trees were more than just a country tree. Widely planted in cities, they shaded many streets. While city dwellers benefited from the trees' beauty, people everywhere also relied on them in another way, perhaps without realizing it. Tannin, the chemical that slows the decay of wood, is used to tan leather. In the late 1800s, America's leather industry treated more than half the leather it produced with tannins extracted from the bark and wood of chestnut trees. In a sense, anyone who wore leather goods "knew" the American chestnut.

During the 1800s, people streamed from the eastern half of the United States into the western territories already occupied by Mexicans and American Indians. These newcomers relentlessly pushed the boundary of the United States to the Pacific coast. As they did, the wood from American chestnut trees was a crucial part of the expanding nation's infrastructure. Because it was rot resistant, it was the preferred wood for railroad ties and telegraph poles, components of the new technologies that connected distant regions of the growing country. The invention of the telephone spurred further demand for chestnut logs because they were used for telephone poles, too.

American chestnut trees were also important to animals. The nutritious nuts filled the bellies of bears, deer, squirrels, chipmunks, raccoons, mice, and voles. Birds—crows, blue jays, and wild turkeys—ate them, too. When the blight arrived, it dealt a serious blow to the forests' food chain. As much as 34% of the nuts these creatures had been eating vanished. Imagine how it would be if you went to a grocery store and discovered that more than one-third of the food you normally ate had disappeared.

When autumn arrived, vendors lined the streets of large cities and sold fresh-roasted chestnuts to passersby.

Because it touched so many different lives, the chestnut tree was an American icon.

And then as the 19th century drew to a close, a tiny invader piggybacked its way across the Pacific Ocean from Asia to the United States. Silently, the fungus that Merkel and Murrill encountered at the zoological park spread from plant nurseries into parks and gardens, to city streets, and finally into forests. In less than 50 years, nearly four billion American chestnut trees became brittle skeletons. Singlehandedly, this small trouble-maker, called the chestnut blight, changed the environment of North America's eastern forests and disrupted the lives of countless people and animals.

Try as they might, no one could conquer the blight. Then scientists had an idea: If someone could locate the original source of the fungus, maybe it would provide clues on what could be done to stop it.

The chestnut blight completely devastated this once-vibrant grove of chestnut trees.

CHAPTER THREE

SEEKING THE SOURCE

Zeroing in on the source of the blight wasn't easy. There are four main species of chestnut trees in the world—the American, the Chinese, the European, and the Japanese. Each of these species has distinctive characteristics that separate it from the other three. The American chestnut is the only chestnut tree native to North America. During colonial times, planters had brought European chestnut trees to North America and crossbred them with American chestnuts. No reports of a chestnut blight had followed the arrival of those trees. From that, scientists concluded that the blight had not come from Europe.

The undersides of Chinese chestnut leaves have tiny hairs (left); American chestnut leaves (below, left) do not.

In the late 1800s, chestnut growers and botanists began importing Japanese chestnut trees to the United States. Their intentions were good—the Japanese chestnut produces larger nuts than the American chestnut. Planters crossbred the two species, hoping their young would produce larger chestnuts with the sweeter flavor of American chestnuts. By 1900,

Chinese chestnuts often have a pair of tiny leaves that grow where each large leaf is attached to a twig or branch. American chestnut trees do not have these tiny leaves.

Chinese chestnut trees had also been imported for a similar reason. The blight appeared within a few years of the Asian chestnut trees' arrival. So it seemed likely that the fungus had originated in Asia. The next task was to prove it.

OFF TO CHINA

Frank Meyer loved traveling all over the world in search of interesting plants.

Frank Meyer, who was born in the Netherlands, loved plants and hiking. He told his parents that he would travel the world and study plants when he grew up. As a teen, Meyer worked at Amsterdam's botanical garden, where he spent hours kneeling on the ground to examine plants and insects. His coworkers chuckled about the dirt that often caked the knees of Meyer's pants. But it wasn't long before Meyer knew more about plants than most other gardeners.

Meyer immigrated to the United States in 1901 and was soon hired by the United States Department of Agriculture (USDA) as an agricultural explorer, a person

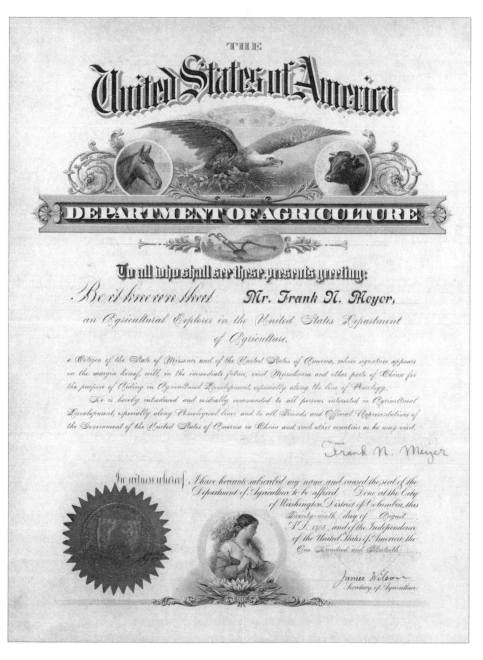

This certificate authorized Frank Meyer to be an explorer on behalf of the United States Department of Agriculture. He may have carried it with him when he visited China.

who traveled abroad in search of new plants and seeds. The job was tailor-made for Meyer. "There goes nothing above fresh air, a blue sky above one's head, and if some mountains or lakes can be added, then life is worth living. I love exploring better than anything else."

In 1913, Meyer set off on an expedition to China. He planned to reexamine a grove of Chinese chestnut trees he'd seen during a previous visit and look for signs of the blight. Meyer had brought a specimen of the blight fungus with him to compare with any fungi he might find. After weeks of hiking through forests, he found the trees. Immediately, he noticed wounds similar to those found on blight-stricken American chestnut trees. But unlike the American trees, the Chinese trees had not died. Although the wounds, called cankers, were huge and unsightly, the trees otherwise appeared healthy.

Meyer collected specimens of the fungus that was growing on the Chinese trees and mailed them to plant pathologists, scientists who study plant diseases, in the United States. It was the same fungus! This satisfied scientists that the blight fungus had originated in Asia.

When two or more species live together for many generations—especially when one of them preys on the other, as the blight fungus does on chestnut trees—the species under threat often adapts, undergoing changes in its genetic makeup. Since Chinese and Japanese chestnut trees could live even when infected with the blight, the scientists reached another conclusion: Asian chestnut trees had adapted to the harmful effects of the blight fungus in a way that enabled them to survive.

HOPE?

By 1940, the loss of nearly four billion American chestnut trees had had far-reaching effects. In a forest, a single mature tree could produce as many as 6,000 nuts a year. That vanished as a food source. Woodland creatures that couldn't adapt to a different food starved. Commercial chestnut growers were forced to grow a different species of chestnut, or to grow hybrid trees, which were produced by breeding two different species of chestnut trees to each other.

The wood from dead trees was usable, but the supply dwindled as sawyers harvested it. In 1899, the lumber industry cut 906.7 million board feet of American chestnut. That number plummeted to 84.7 million board feet in 1943, and only 4.4 million in 1960. Similarly, the use of chestnut for railroad ties fell from

Even though the chestnut blight killed trees, the wood was still useful. The timber industry harvested the dead trees for their valuable lumber.

approximately 8 million ties in 1908 to 115,000 in 1931. As a result of the blight, telephone, telegraph, and electric companies discontinued the use of American chestnut poles, which in 1928 accounted for more than 25% of all the poles purchased. They switched to less durable woods that, unlike chestnut poles, had to be treated with preservatives to prevent rot. By the late 1950s, obtaining tannin from American chestnut trees for tanning leather was out of the question.

Had the death knell rung for the once-mighty tree? It seemed so—in fact, many people believed that it had become extinct. But that was not true.

The roots of many American chestnut trees are still living beneath the soil. Certain microbes in the soil stop the blight fungus from invading the buried roots. The healthy roots continually send up new sprouts that ring the lifeless stump. Each sprout develops its own root system and becomes a sapling. But its reprieve from the blight is only temporary. The sapling grows for 5 to 10 years, until eventually the blight kills it.

Unfortunately, these roots can't restore chestnut trees to their former position as forest giants. Biologist Martin Cipollini is a college professor who studies and breeds chestnut trees in Georgia. He lamented, "The old stumps won't sprout indefinitely. It's like a bank account. You can keep making withdrawals, but unless you make new deposits, the money will eventually run out. Lavender Mountain, in Georgia, used to be covered with American chestnut shoots. During a recent search, we only found two."

But scientists haven't given up the fight. When it comes to scientific research, the adage "Don't put all your eggs in one basket" is wise advice. Researchers frequently experiment with several different methods in their quest to achieve a certain goal. If one approach fails, all is not lost. If more than one method succeeds, a

wider variety of solutions can be applied. Breeding the kind of American chestnut tree that everyone wants and successfully restoring it to our forests may require using more than one method.

Scientists are currently trying three different approaches. One pits an even tinier foe against the blight fungus. Another uses a tried-and-true method of crossbreeding chestnut species. The third approach requires cutting-edge scientific technology.

Thin new stems will continue to sprout from the tree's roots long after the large trunk dies.

CHAPTER FOUR

AN EYEBROW-
RAISING
DISCOVERY

ALTHOUGH SCIENTISTS HAD LEARNED THE BLIGHT'S source, that didn't stop American chestnut trees from getting sick and dying. Even worse, during the 1930s the blight spread across the Atlantic Ocean to Europe, where it began to attack European chestnut trees. But just when widespread devastation seemed certain, something unexpected happened. Some of the sick trees got better!

In the mid-1960s, French scientist Jean Grente examined many of these trees and noticed something odd. The color of the fungus on the healed trees was white. On dying and dead trees, it was bright orange, the color usually seen on blight-infected trees in America. It seemed that there might be more than one strain, or kind, of the blight fungus, and one was weaker than the other. But Grente had no idea why.

Scientists wondered why some European chestnut trees survived the blight.

A SICK FUNGUS

In 1972, Sandra Anagnostakis and Peter Day at the Connecticut Agricultural Experiment Station (CAES) were determined to find out what made Grente's white fungus different. They tested samples of the white fungus that Grente had sent them and soon discovered a crucial difference between the orange and the white strains. America's orange, harmful strain of the fungus produced a lot of oxalic acid, a substance that in large amounts kills plants. When the deadly strain of the fungus attacked a chestnut tree, it introduced a mighty dose of oxalic acid into the cambium. There, the acid dissolved the molecular bonds between the cells that formed the tree's tissue. After the acid broke the bonds, the blight fungus devoured the cells' contents. Then it rapidly spread throughout the cambium in a cell-by-cell chain reaction of destruction that would eventually kill the tree.

In comparison, Grente's weak strains of the fungus produced very little oxalic acid. Without its lethal dose of oxalic acid, the blight fungus was like a rattlesnake without venom. Chestnuts trees infected with the weak fungus continued living.

This partially explained why some European chestnut trees survived the blight. But Anagnostakis and Day

Sandra Anagnostakis and her colleagues at the CAES have devoted years to studying the blight fungus and its effects on chestnut trees.

knew there had to be more to it. What made some strains of the fungus produce less oxalic acid?

FUNGUS FIGHTS

When the CAES scientists microscopically examined the fungal strains, they made a startling discovery: The weak strains of the fungus were sick! All the European chestnut trees that had survived did so because the strain of the blight that attacked them had caught a virus. The virus weakened the blight fungus in the same way a virus such as the flu weakens you. Unlike the deadly strain of the fungus, whose powerful punch of oxalic acid quickly attacked the tree, the weak strain spread much more slowly. That gave the trees time to activate their immune systems to fight the blight. They produced a type of cell that formed a gnarly ridge of bark around each canker. This barrier walled off the fungus and prevented it from spreading. Since the fungus could not girdle the tree, nutrients still flowed, and the tree didn't die. Although their bark was scarred, the survivors grew new, healthy branches and still produced bountiful crops of nuts.

GOING VIRAL

Viruses are microscopic particles. The word *virus* comes from Latin, meaning "poison." They are not scientifically classified as plants, animals, or fungi. They cannot reproduce until they are inside the cell of a living organism, such as a plant, an animal, or, in the case of the chestnut blight, a fungus. After a virus gets inside a cell, it multiplies. Often, this sickens the plant or animal. In people, viruses cause diseases such as chicken pox, the flu, and some colds. Viruses spread from one organism to another through the air, in water or body fluids, through insect bites, or through skin contact.

The cells of living organisms contain molecules of an acid called deoxyribonucleic acid (DNA). Some viruses have DNA, but others contain a different acid—which humans also have—called ribonucleic acid (RNA). The viruses that can infect the blight fungus have RNA. These viruses' RNA causes changes in the blight fungus's DNA in a way that weakens the fungus.

Sometimes the blight fungus changes color from orange to white after a virus weakens it. But this doesn't always happen. Sometimes the only way that scientists can tell if the fungus is infected is by testing it to see if it contains a virus's RNA.

Armed with this knowledge, European scientists began a bold experiment. They scraped cankers caused by the deadly strain and exposed the tissue beneath. Then they smeared a weak strain of the fungus into the wounds. The scientists hoped the super-harmful fungus would catch the virus from the weaker one and become a milder form of the blight, one that chestnut trees could survive.

The results perplexed them. Sometimes the deadly fungus caught the virus and the tree healed. Other times it didn't and the tree died.

Anagnostakis and her colleagues tackled this new puzzle by growing colonies of deadly blight fungus in the CAES laboratory. When the colonies had matured, the researchers inoculated (deliberately infected) them with weak strains of the fungus. They got the same mixed results that the European scientists had.

Microscopic examination of the fungal tissue samples provided the answer. Success or failure in making the strong fungus catch a virus depended on the spaghetti-like threads that each fungus sent out as it grew. Every time the virus was transmitted to the more harmful fungus, the threads of the weak strain had fused with those of the deadly strain. When the threads had not fused, the virus was not transmitted. From this, the scientists realized that the tissues of different strains of the fungus aren't always compatible. A similar

The trunks of these young chestnut trees may not look glamorous, but the lumpy bulges are marks of success: These trees survived weak strains of the blight.

reaction sometimes occurs in human organ transplants. When an organ is donated, the tissue of the donated organ—a liver or kidney, for example—must be compatible with that of the recipient. If it isn't, the recipient's body rejects the donated organ. When blight fungus tissues are incompatible, they will not fuse. That stops the virus from being passed along; the mega-harmful fungus remains strong and the tree dies.

When the CAES scientists were ready to inoculate trees in their orchards with weak strains of the blight fungus, they had to find a way to be sure the fungi's tissues were compatible. To avoid failure due to tissue incompatibility, the researchers included a mixture of different weak strains in each inoculation. That increased the likelihood that at least some of the tissue threads would be compatible and fuse.

As soon as a blight canker appeared on a tree in their orchard, the team inoculated it with the mixture. They treated all the cankers for four years and then stopped treatment, waiting to see what would happen. During that time, bugs and other creatures crawled over and brushed against the cankers. Spores from the inoculated fungus stuck to their feet, fur, and feathers. They carried these spores with them until the spores dropped off and found their way into cankers on other chestnut trees. Slowly, the weak strains spread.

Much to the scientists' satisfaction, the trees whose fungus caught the virus did not die. Although some of them died back to the ground, their roots survived and re-sprouted. More encouraging, others never died back.

Dead branches poked from their leafy crowns, and unsightly healed cankers dotted their trunks, but despite their raggedy appearance, these hardy survivors produced heavy crops of nuts. The weak strains of the blight fungus introduced more than 30 years ago have now spread throughout the CAES orchards, and new cankers that develop begin healing on their own.

Many of the chestnut trees in the CAES orchards are hardy specimens that generate new growth and regularly produce nuts.

But another important thing that Anagnostakis and her colleagues learned from their experiments was that some American chestnuts are better survivors than others.

CHAPTER FIVE
MIDWESTERN SURVIVORS

ON A WINTRY DAY IN EARLY 1976, Priscilla Johnson decided to go cross-country skiing near her home in Michigan. As she slid through the woods, she came upon a group of small trees that caught her interest. Cankers, the telltale sign of the blight, marred their trunks. The trees were, however, very much alive. Prickly brown burs—proof of life from the previous autumn—still hung on some of the branches.

The previous year, Johnson had read a newspaper article about the CAES scientists and their work with weak strains of the blight fungus. First, she was curious to know if the trees she'd found were American chestnut trees. If so, they were growing outside the normal range of these trees. During the 18th and 19th centuries, settlers who moved west had often brought chestnut seeds with them. If the trees Johnson had seen were American chestnuts, it was likely that they were descendants of those trees. She was surprised that the trees seemed to be surviving the blight and wondered if that might be because they had a weak strain of the blight. To find out, she sent a piece of healed bark to the CAES.

The scientists examined 11 samples that Johnson sent over time. They were elated to find that about half of them did, in fact, contain a virus. This meant that Michigan had its own native weak strain of the blight fungus! "It's the only place in North America where American chestnut trees have recovered on their own from the blight," exclaimed plant pathologist Dennis Fulbright, who has studied the Michigan trees for many years. "There are differences between the Michigan and European [virus-weakened] strains. One difference is that our strain doesn't change its color. Even when infected, the fungus stays orange." But the scientists knew that the virus was present because when they examined the orange fungus under a microscope, they found the virus's genetic material—its RNA—inside it.

Scientists and chestnut growers started inoculating blight-stricken orchards in Michigan with Michigan's weak strain of the blight. Out of 50 trees treated, the cankers on 38 of them healed. Despite having dead crowns, healthy new branches covered with lush green leaves grew in the middle portions of the trees. These encouraging signs led chestnut scientists to wonder if Michigan's weak strain could help blight-stricken American chestnut trees elsewhere.

WISCONSIN HOLDOUTS

Farmer Martin Hicks was one of the settlers who had planted American chestnut seeds when he moved west in the early 1900s. Even though the trees he planted on his farm near West Salem, Wisconsin, were more than 350 miles west of their native range, they thrived in Wisconsin's hilly countryside. By the 1970s, the descendants of these trees had multiplied into a forest of more than 3,000 trees. And they were strong, healthy, and blight-free. When word spread of the remarkable stand (group) of trees, scientists and others interested in the American chestnut traveled from all parts of the United States to see them.

It wasn't long before the killer fungus found West Salem. Perhaps it flew in on the wings of birds from the east or was tramped in on the shoes of eager

The owners of the West Salem stand of chestnut trees didn't want their magnificent trees to die. They finally decided that inoculation might be the best way to save them.

visitors. Regardless of how it arrived, by the late 1980s, the land's owners, Ron Bockenhauer and Delores Rhyme, saw wilted yellow leaves, the first sign of the blight.

Experts inspected the trees and offered suggestions. The landowners sprayed, cut down, and burned many of the diseased trees, as people had when the blight first appeared in the early 1900s. Even so, tree after tree sickened. Finally, Bockenhauer and Rhyme decided to let scientists treat the trees with weak strains of the blight fungus. Maybe that would help their trees recover.

Before the scientists inoculated the trees, they analyzed samples of the West Salem fungus from multiple cankers and found that it was genetically identical throughout the stand. They needed to be sure, however, that the virus would spread easily from one tree to another. In a laboratory, the scientists inoculated samples of the deadly West Salem fungus with several weakened strains, each containing a different virus. One weak strain outperformed the rest—the one with the Michigan virus.

Inoculating all of West Salem's 3,000 trees was a job too large for the scientists and their team of volunteer helpers. Instead, in 1992 they inoculated cankers on select trees in test plots established within the stand. They hoped Michigan's weak strain would spread from

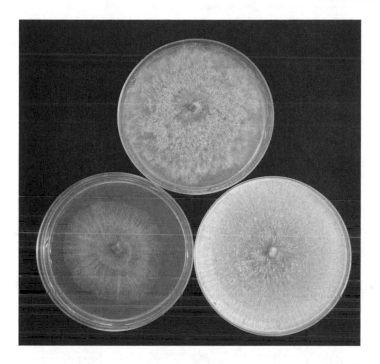

Top: The deadly strain of the blight fungus in West Salem as it appears before it has been infected with a virus.
Bottom left: The West Salem fungus infected with Michigan's virus-weakened strain. Bottom right: The West Salem fungus infected with a European blight fungus that was weakened by a virus.

the inoculated cankers to untreated cankers on the same tree, and then to untreated trees.

Unfortunately, it didn't. The spread of the inoculated West Salem fungus was hampered because the virus wasn't being passed along in the deadly fungus's reproductive cells.

Inoculating the West Salem trees with a different virus-infected strain, one from Italy, partly solved the problem. The Italian strain didn't weaken the

The holes bored into this trunk surround a canker. Each one has been filled with a virus-weakened strain of the blight fungus.

West Salem deadly fungus as much as the Michigan strain had, but it produced a lot more spores that contained the virus. Encouragingly, the weak Italian strain spread to some of the new cankers that formed on the inoculated trees. Discouragingly, the strain did not appear to spread to untreated trees, which had been a major goal.

Meanwhile, the blight spread to healthy trees. At the same time, new cankers on the treated trees rapidly developed. The team of inoculators couldn't keep up with the outbreak. In 1998, the frustrated team suspended all inoculations and waited to see what would happen. By 2004, the weak strain still hadn't spread as hoped. It seemed that the West Salem trees were doomed.

Still, the discouraged scientists didn't give up. Recovery for a long-lived species like the American chestnut can take years, often longer than a human lifetime. In 2004 scientists resumed the inoculation treatment with the Italian weak strain. This time, continued treatment and patience seem to be paying off. Since 2008 the weak strain has slowly become established in the test plots. Scientists are cautiously optimistic about the prospects of the trees that have been treated for the longest amount of time. Many of them have healed cankers—a survivor's badge of honor. Their crowns have new branches and healthy leaves and, most encouraging of all, the trees are producing

The owners and the scientists were glad to see this healed canker. This encouraging sign gives them hope that the West Salem stand may survive.

nuts. But the West Salem trees aren't out of danger yet. Will their recovery continue? Only time will tell.

Even before the scientists began their inoculation program in West Salem, others were hard at work trying to overcome the blight with a second approach. They hoped to breed blight-resistant American chestnut trees.

CHAPTER SIX

IT'S IN THE GENES

By the time Fred Hebard was born in 1948, the heyday of the American chestnut tree was long gone. In fact, if some young cows hadn't escaped from their pasture, Hebard might not have ever met the tree. On a break from his college studies, Hebard was working for Herman Weingart Jr., a Connecticut farmer. One day, several heifers wandered off into the woods, so the two men hiked after them. "During our walk, we came across an American chestnut tree," Hebard recalled. That's when Weingart told him the story of the chestnut blight. "A fleeting thought crossed my mind—before we returned to the task of tracking down those pesky heifers—that it would be nice to return to college, study biology, and cure the chestnut blight," said Hebard. That fleeting thought grew into a career goal of becoming a plant pathologist. As Hebard worked toward that goal, he discovered that curing the blight was far more difficult than he'd ever imagined. "My expectation at first was that the task could be accomplished quickly. I gradually learned it was a lifetime proposition. But it was good for me because it gave me a mission." Hebard knew that the CAES and others were attempting to spread weak strains of the blight fungus. But he was interested in trying something else. He hoped to grow American chestnut trees that were blight resistant.

Years before, when it had become clear that the blight was wiping out American chestnut trees, growers had started chestnut breeding programs. Again and again, USDA scientists had bred pure American chestnut trees from one area of the United States with those from another, hoping that some of the baby trees would be blight resistant. Their efforts failed.

Later, scientists at the Brooklyn Botanic Garden and at the CAES tried something different: They crossbred American trees with Chinese and Japanese chestnut trees. This produced baby trees that were half American chestnut and half Asian chestnut.

DNA is how the instructions for forming and sustaining life are passed from one generation to the next.

*One side of this image depicts the shape of a mature
American chestnut tree as it appears in summer; the other side shows
the tree's leafless wintertime appearance.*

Spores produced by mature colonies of the chestnut blight fungus create small orange bumps that dot the bark of infected trees.

At TACF's farms, crews working to inoculate trees carry containers stocked with boring tools, tape, spatulas, and petri dishes that contain two different strains of the fungus.

The blight fungus in this petri dish has been "punched" with a boring tool to create the small plugs that will be inserted into wounds on the trees that are being inoculated.

With care, this tiny clump of transgenic American chestnut embryos can be regenerated into beautiful, blight-resistant trees.
[Linda Polin-McGuigan]

The metal collar protects young seedlings from deer and rodents. Each seedling is labeled with a tag that contains information about its history.

Many hundreds of chestnut seedlings have succumbed to the blight at TACF's farms. But the sixth generation trees show encouraging blight resistance. Hopefully most of these sixth generation seedlings will survive and be transplanted to grow elsewhere.

When catkins are immature, their flowers are tightly closed. The pollen they contain is not yet ready to fertilize female flowers.

Pollen from mature chestnut catkins like these can fertilize the female flowers that grow on other chestnut trees.

Mature catkins on the crown of an American chestnut tree look like miniature cream-colored fireworks.

During the weeks after a tiny bur has been fertilized, the nuts inside will grow until the bur becomes larger than a golf ball.

The spines on the outside of a mature bur are sharper than a needle!

It wasn't long before the nuts contained in this bur fell to the ground.
[The Connecticut Agricultural Experiment Station]

*A male eastern towhee calls from his perch on the sprout
of an American chestnut tree.*
[Photo courtesy of MassWildlife/Bill Byrne]

The texture of a tree's bark is determined by its genes. See how the bark on birch, silver maple, and chestnut trees does not look alike.

The molecules in DNA are made of units called genes. Genes transmit information that codes for traits that offspring can inherit from their parents. In humans, particular genes determine characteristics such as hair and eye colors. A chestnut tree's genes determine its leaf shape and bark texture. More important for chestnut breeders, Asian chestnut trees have certain genes that enable them to fend off the blight. These are the genes that chestnut breeders needed in order to grow a blight-resistant tree. American chestnut trees lack these genes, but some of the babies crossbred at the CAES inherited blight resistance from their Asian parent trees. These lucky babies survived when the blight attacked them.

MOTHERS AND FATHERS

Male and *female* may not be the first words that come to mind when you think about trees, yet to their offspring, trees are exactly that. Flowers are a tree's reproductive organs. Many trees have flowers that contain both male and female parts. Others, including chestnuts, have separate male and female flowers on the same tree. Pollen from male flowers produced by some species of trees can pollinate female flowers on the same tree. But pollen from one chestnut tree must be transported to the female flower of another chestnut tree to make a baby chestnut tree. Depending on which flower a scientist uses for breeding, a tree can be either a mother or a father.

An immature catkin's buds are tightly closed.

A chestnut tree's male flowers are produced on a catkin, which is 4 to 10 inches long and looks like a fuzzy caterpillar. The tiny cream-colored blossoms coat the catkin from the beginning to the middle of summer. These flowers produce pollen, the tree's male reproductive cell, but the DNA in pollen contains only half the genetic material that a chestnut tree needs to produce a nut.

DNA from the female flower of another tree supplies the other half. Female chestnut flowers grow in clusters embedded in a bur, a prickly green ball about one-third of an inch long that grows near the base of a catkin. Each bur contains the tree's female reproductive cells. Like pollen, those cells

After this female flower is fertilized, it will produce three chestnuts.

contain only half of the genetic information needed to pro-duce a nut.

When pollen fertilizes the female reproductive cells, the DNA from both parent trees combines and provides all the genetic information needed to produce a chestnut seed—the nut. Nuts develop only after this happens. Each nut pro-duced receives one half of its genes from its mother and one half from its father, just as you did from your parents.

When plant growers breed chestnut trees, they remove pollen from the father tree and use it to fertilize select flowers on a different mother tree. To make sure that these flowers are fertilized with pollen only from the chosen father tree, as soon as the flower appears, it is covered with a small bag. This prevents the pol-len of other chestnut trees that is carried by the wind or insects from landing on the flower.

A fully mature American chestnut bur is about the size of a golf ball and usually contains three nuts.

When the nuts are mature, the bur opens and the nuts fall to the ground.

Even though some of the babies grown at the Brooklyn Botanic Garden and the CAES were blight resistant, growers elsewhere weren't satisfied. American chestnut trees were valued for their straight, single trunks, which are ideal for the timber trade. This characteristic is determined by their genes. Asian chestnut trees are usually multi-stemmed. Many of the cross-bred baby trees that survived the blight had inherited the genes for multi-stemmed trunks, so they weren't as useful for lumber.

A difficult task faced growers who wanted the single-trunk kind of tree. Could they breed trees that had the Asian genes for blight resistance *and* the American chestnut's genes for a straight trunk? A group of plant growers hoped that a modified method of crossbreeding would achieve that goal.

A TRIED-AND-TRUE BREEDING PLAN

College professor Charles Burnham specialized in breeding corn plants. But he was always willing to learn something new, and the plight of the American chestnut captivated him. In 1983, Burnham, along with a group of plant scientists and chestnut grower Philip Rutter, founded The American Chestnut Foundation

(TACF), an organization dedicated to saving and restoring the tree to North American forests. They believed that a long-established plant-breeding method called backcross breeding (which Burnham had used to breed corn) might solve the American chestnut's blight troubles. They hoped to naturally transfer the blight-resistance genes from Asian chestnut trees into future generations of American chestnut trees.

Their plan required fields for growing trees and time for them to grow, so in 1989, TACF established the Wagner Research Farm in Meadowview, Virginia. TACF hired Fred Hebard to supervise the backcross-breeding program. On April 15, 1989, Hebard, Rutter, and about 80 volunteers—who ranged in age from 3 years old to 90—planted about 300 young trees. The seedlings came from nurseries in Florida, Kentucky, Ohio, Minnesota, Iowa, and as far west as Washington and Oregon. Some were pure American chestnut; many were Chinese chestnut or their hybrids. The next year, they planted about 1,000 nuts. These were the first two of many plantings on the gently sloping hills of Wagner Research Farm.

Other troubles struck before the blight did: Rodents gnawed the seedlings' stems; browsing deer ate the leaves. Scientists and volunteers rescued the endangered plants by wrapping a protective metal tube around each seedling. During droughts, they watered the growing trees.

An animal, perhaps a vole (below), girdled the
stem of this seedling. This damage stops nutrients
from flowing in the tree's cambium.

By 2014, three more farms had been added to TACF's research grounds. Together they were home to 40,000 chestnut trees. But the backcross-breeding program couldn't move into full swing until the seedlings planted in 1989 had matured and flowered, which took about three years. To be sure the babies would inherit a lot of American chestnut genes, one parent tree was always a pure American chestnut.

The babies of these trees were the first generation of the TACF breeding program's trees, and like the ones grown at the CAES, half of their genes were American chestnut and half were Chinese chestnut.

The next task was to breed more generations of blight-resistant trees but to make them as much like American chestnut trees as possible. The goal was to keep the Asian tree's blight-resistance genes while replacing its unwanted genes—like those that made the trees multi-stemmed—with the desired American chestnut genes. That's where backcrossing entered the picture.

After the half-American–half-Chinese chestnut seedlings matured and produced flowers, each became a parent for the second generation. The other parent was always a pure American chestnut tree. That way, the babies would have more American chestnut genes than the previous generation had; instead of being half American, they would be three-quarters American and one-quarter Chinese. This is called backcross breeding

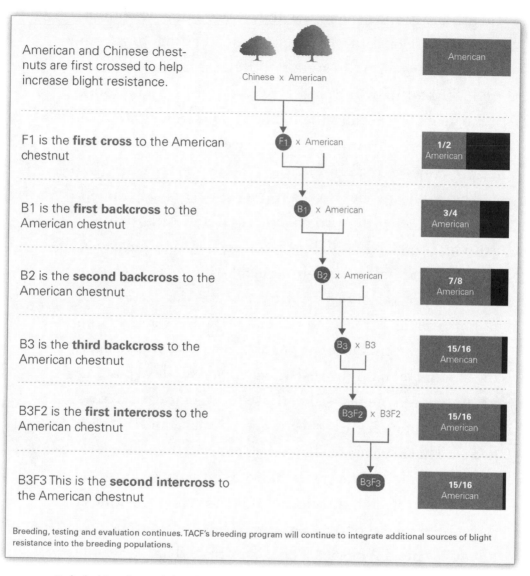

American and Chinese chestnuts are first crossed to help increase blight resistance.

Chinese × American

American

F1 is the **first cross** to the American chestnut

F1 × American

1/2 American

B1 is the **first backcross** to the American chestnut

B1 × American

3/4 American

B2 is the **second backcross** to the American chestnut

B2 × American

7/8 American

B3 is the **third backcross** to the American chestnut

B3 × B3

15/16 American

B3F2 is the **first intercross** to the American chestnut

B3F2 × B3F2

15/16 American

B3F3 This is the **second intercross** to the American chestnut

B3F3

15/16 American

Breeding, testing and evaluation continues. TACF's breeding program will continue to integrate additional sources of blight resistance into the breeding populations.

Only babies that exhibit the desired characteristics of the American chestnut and demonstrate blight resistance are chosen for further breeding. An intercross occurs when two babies that contain the desired American chestnut genes and the blight resistant Asian chestnut genes are bred to one another. Both must be 15/16 American chestnut.

because the breeders choose—go back to—a pure American chestnut tree as one of the parent trees for the first three generations. The other parent is a matured baby from the previous generation that has the characteristics the scientists want. With this breeding method, the number of American chestnut genes in each new generation increases, and the Chinese chestnut genes decrease.

A chestnut tree has about 40,000 genes. Babies produced by the sixth generation with backcross breeding contain about 37,500 American chestnut genes and about 2,500 Chinese chestnut genes. Sixth-generation trees are practically indistinguishable from pure American chestnuts with one exception: They can resist the blight.

But how do Hebard and his colleagues know which babies in each generation will be the most blight resistant and have the desired characteristics of the American chestnut?

SMALL DIFFERENCES

All the people on earth are humans—*Homo sapiens*—but we are not exact copies of each other. If you compared your DNA with a friend's, you would find similarities and differences. The same would be true if you compared the American chestnut trees growing in one location with those from another. The variation that occurs within a group of living organisms—people, trees, dogs—is called genetic diversity.

If disease threatens a group of organisms, the group's genetic diversity could make the difference between those organisms' survival and extinction. The American chestnut is a perfect example. It doesn't naturally have genes that resist the blight fungus. In this respect, these trees are all similar—not diverse. As a result, all pure American chestnuts die when the blight attacks them.

But in other ways, American chestnut trees are diverse. They grow in several different climates. In Maine, they withstand frigid winters. In Georgia, they survive sweltering summers. Some regions are wetter than others. And the soil composition varies from state to state. Small variations in the American chestnut trees' genes—their genetic diversity—have allowed them to live in a wide variety of environments.

TACF scientists want to be sure that the blight-resistant trees they produce can live in different regions and conditions, not just in the climate and environmental conditions in Virginia. That requires genetic diversity. To get this diversity, the scientists are using American chestnut trees from different regions in their backcrosses. This keeps a constant flow of new and varied genes blending into each generation. "Our near-term goal is to produce trees capable of surviving and reproducing in our forests so they can resume evolving on their own," explained plant pathologist Laura Georgi.

SURVIVAL OF THE FITTEST

It would take years of planting chestnut seeds and waiting to see which babies naturally catch the blight and which ones don't. So to speed up the process, scientists deliberately inoculate each new generation of seedlings with the blight fungus. They do this by boring two small holes in the trunk of each young tree,

Boring a small hole into the tree's stem provides an opening where researchers can insert the blight fungus.

just deep enough to expose the cambium. One hole is inoculated with a weak strain of the blight fungus; the other hole is inoculated with the more deadly one. Two strains of the blight fungus are used so the scientists can quickly tell if a seedling is weakly or strongly blight resistant. Masking tape wrapped around the two wounds keeps the fungi from drying out and sliding out of the holes. Workers on TACF's farms document what happens to every tree that has been planted.

A few months after a tree is inoculated, a crew returns to the fields and checks the inoculation sites. By then, the least blight-resistant trees have already died. Others may have the blight fungus's pinhead-sized orange bumps. Some have developed cankers. A crew member measures these gnarly wounds—which often grow very large—and records any changes.

Over the next year or two, scientists discover which trees will survive. Dead and dying trees are removed. Only blight-resistant trees are used for further breeding. After several years, the surviving young trees—even if they have unsightly cankers— are considered the hardiest chestnut trees of their backcrossed generations. But even then, only the young trees that have blight resistance *and* the desired characteristics of an American chestnut are selected for further breeding. These are the trees that the scientists eventually want to restore in forests.

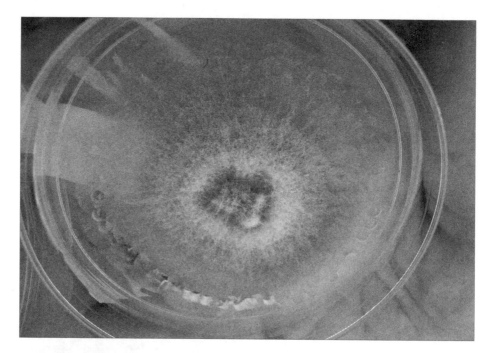

Above: Each circle-shaped plug punched along the edge of this blight fungus colony contains enough material to infect a chestnut tree. Below left: A volunteer transfers the plug with a small spatula. Below: The plug is inserted directly into the wound on the trunk.

In 2005, 16 years after the establishment of TACF's Virginia farms, Hebard's crew of scientists and volunteers harvested the nuts (about 100) of the trees that TACF believed were suitable for forest restoration projects. They named these sixth-generation trees Restoration Chestnut 1.0. (*Sixth generation* means that the Restoration Chestnut 1.0 trees were the great-great-great-great-grandchildren of the original mother and father trees.) In 2009, the first Restoration Chestnut 1.0 seedlings were planted in select forests. How well

All of these young trees have been inoculated with the blight fungus. Time will reveal which ones are blight resistant.

Fred Hebard demonstrates how a bag will be fastened around a fertilized bur.

they will succeed in the long term is still being determined.

Even as trees continued to be inoculated with weak strains of the blight and backcross-breeding programs were producing babies, another group of scientists had started on a third approach to combating the blight. Their quest for a blight-resistant American chestnut applies a different method of reproducing trees—one that requires pioneering scientific technology.

*Bags have been securely fastened around select female
flowers to prevent undesired pollen from fertilizing them.*

CHAPTER SEVEN

HIGH-TECH ARMOR

LINDA MCGUIGAN IS A FOSTER MOTHER. For six weeks, she regularly bathes the babies in her care with an antibiotic to kill anything that could harm them. She nourishes them with special food. The babies live in incubators, in which McGuigan controls the light, temperature, and humidity that surround them. Without round-the-clock care, they will die. When McGuigan receives the babies, they are still embryos— cells that can grow into adults. Each one contains all the genetic material it needs to grow into an American chestnut tree.

CREATING THE SHIELD

Biotechnologists Charles Maynard and William Powell work at the State University of New York's College of Environmental Science and Forestry in Syracuse. Since the 1990s, they, McGuigan, and a team of colleagues have been raising American chestnut tree seedlings armed with a built-in blight-fighting shield.

The shield isn't made of metal, though. Instead, it's made of a substance found in wheat. Wheat's DNA has genes that make the plant produce oxalate oxidase— scientists call it OxO for short. Chestnut growers like OxO because it breaks down oxalic acid, the acid that blight fungi use to destroy a chestnut tree's cells.

In Maynard's laboratory, the scientists remove OxO genes from the DNA of wheat. Then, using a special technique, they transfer the OxO genes into the DNA of an American chestnut tree. Because the trees they raise contain genes that have been transferred from a different plant species, they are called transgenic American chestnut trees.

But Maynard and his assistants can't simply squirt the OxO genes just anywhere inside a chestnut tree. For the OxO shield to become a characteristic that is passed from a parent tree to its young, the OxO genes must be inserted into the DNA of a single cell inside each chestnut embryo.

Twelve tiny new baby trees grow in a petri dish.

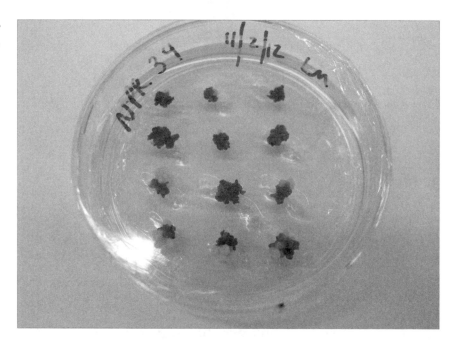

Part of Linda McGuigan's job as an embryo foster mother is making sure that the OxO genes have been successfully transferred into the cells. She monitors them carefully to see that this occurs. But researchers can't control the exact spot where the OxO genes land in each embryo's DNA. They can end up in different places. Because of this, all transgenic American chestnut embryos are not identical.

Maynard and Powell's team adds only one to four genes to the DNA of a pure American chestnut. The embryo is then about 99.99% American chestnut. (The sixth-generation backcross trees bred at TACF's farms in Virginia, in contrast, are about 93.75% American chestnut, with the rest being Asian chestnut genes.) After the OxO genes are in place, the embryo is ready to become the first tree in a line, or succession, of trees that contain the OxO blight-fighting shield.

FRAGILE BABIES

A transgenic embryo's survival is not guaranteed. Under normal growing conditions, the nut's hard hull, or shell, protects the embryo growing inside. Transgenic embryos do not have this hull shelter because scientists have to remove it to insert the OxO genes. For this reason, McGuigan protects the embryos by creating an environment as similar as possible to being inside a chestnut hull. She supplies the embryos with the sugars, salts, and nutrients typically found in soil. The embryos are protected, but despite antibiotic baths, contaminants sometimes sneak in. When they do, many of the embryos die.

McGuigan nourishes the survivors with hormones, special substances that stimulate growth. As each embryo grows, its color changes from white to greenish brown. Sometimes the embryos look so sickly that McGuigan thinks they're going to die. But then, "just when I don't think anything is going to happen, a tiny green shoot pops out," McGuigan said. That tiny green shoot is what she has been waiting for.

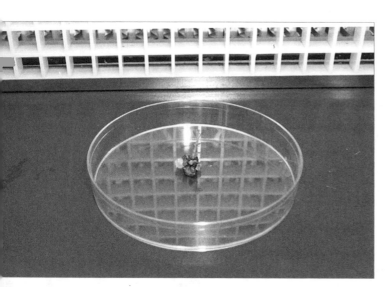

Linda McGuigan waits for a tiny shoot like this to appear.

When an embryo's shoot is about 1½ inches long, McGuigan slices it crosswise into three or four pieces. Each piece contains a small leaf and a tiny bump called a growth node. Each piece continues to grow, and when it reaches 1½ inches, McGuigan again cuts it into segments, as she did earlier. By repeating this process a number of times, she obtains many shoots from just one embryo.

Have you ever pinched a sprig off a houseplant and put it in a glass of water until it grew roots? The new plant you grew has the same genetic makeup as the plant you plucked it from. It is a clone of the parent plant. Each chestnut shoot that McGuigan raises is a clone of the embryo it sprouted from; their genes are identical.

Finally, she allows some of the shoots to grow larger.

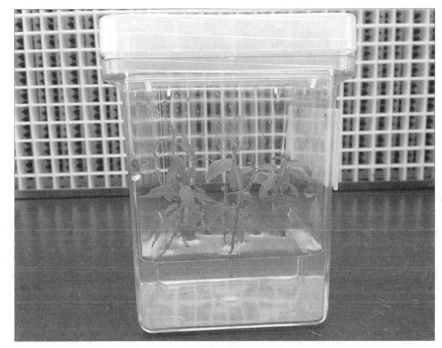

When Allison Oakes first places the small chestnut shoots in a nutrient-filled gel, they have not yet developed roots.

When they are about three inches long, McGuigan passes them on to her colleague Allison Oakes, who treats them with another hormone that stimulates root growth. After several roots appear, Oakes plants each baby in potting soil. But the chestnut seedling can't be planted outside yet; it is still so fragile that it can't even be placed in a regular room.

Baby transgenic American chestnuts need high humidity—much higher than that normally found in a home, school, or laboratory. Many people find very high humidity uncomfortable, but baby transgenic American chestnut trees thrive in it. In fact, they die without it.

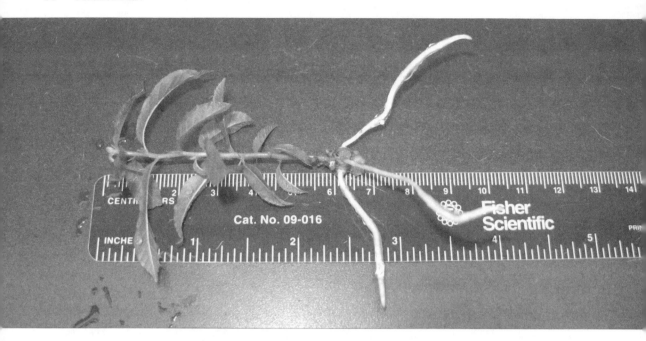

After the shoots have grown several roots, they are ready to be planted in soil-filled containers.

The transgenic seedlings must stay inside a special growth chamber that has extremely high levels of humidity. And that still isn't enough! To add even more humidity, Oakes covers the container of each plant with a plastic bag. An elastic band snapped around the pot's rim holds the bag in place. Each plant's mini-greenhouse adds an extra dose of humidity—just the right amount that the baby needs for survival.

As the babies grow, they produce new leaves that gradually allow them to handle normal amounts of humidity. At that point, the baby trees move into a regular greenhouse, where they grow for several more months. Only when they have a healthy bunch of leaves can they be safely planted outdoors. It takes nearly a year and a half of constant care and supervision to grow a transgenic American chestnut tree from an embryo to an orchard-ready tree.

DOES IT WORK?

Powell and his colleagues have grown many transgenic American chestnut trees. But only an experiment could prove if their work was successful or not.

Powell's team simultaneously grew four sets of chestnut trees. The first and second were transgenic American chestnut trees. The third was a non-transgenic pure American chestnut; the fourth was a Chinese chestnut. The embryos of all four were raised in the same way that the team grew their transgenic trees. In this way, they could tell if the addition of the OxO genes helped their transgenic trees resist the blight.

When the time was right, the scientists inoculated all four seedlings with the blight fungus. They monitored the trees for fifteen days. All the trees developed a canker. The pure American tree (which had no natural blight resistance) developed a large one and died. The canker on the Chinese tree (which has natural blight resistance) grew slightly larger than the wound made for the inoculation, but the tree survived. Those on each of the transgenic trees never spread beyond the wound site; both transgenic trees survived. Clearly, the OxO shield worked.

Inoculating a tree's stem with the blight fungus is a surefire way to see if a tree is blight resistant. But the tree might not show signs of infection for weeks or even

Inoculation results seem clear: The pure American chestnut seedlings (on the left) are dead. The transgenic trees (in the middle), which contain the OxO gene, are thriving. The Chinese chestnuts (on the right) show their typical blight resistance.

months. So Powell and his colleague Andrew Newhouse devised a blight-indicator test that they could use on trees still in the greenhouse. Newhouse inoculated wounds he made on the leaves, rather than on the stems. Although the blight is not a leaf disease, a tender chestnut leaf develops a dark spot around the inoculation site. If the spot grows, the scientists believe that it indicates that the tree is susceptible to the blight. If the spot remains small, it appears the tree is resistant.

While the leaf test is not a guarantee, so far it has consistently predicted which trees are most likely to get the blight. Since the scientists want to produce only the most blight-resistant trees, those that "fail" the leaf test are removed from the program. After the survivors are planted outside, they will be further tested with traditional stem inoculations.

Maynard and Powell's team planted the first transgenic American chestnut trees outdoors in a test plot in June 2006. Since then, more than 1,000 baby trees have been planted in different test plots.

INHERITING THE SHIELD

A huge question still remains: Can transgenic parent trees pass their blight resistance along to their babies?

Because transgenic trees are experimental trees, they are under strict regulation. In fact, it is against the law to breed them freely. The breeding of all transgenic trees must be reported to the USDA's Animal and Plant Health Inspection Service. Until proper approval is granted, it's illegal to let transgenic American chestnut trees release pollen into the air. The transgenic trees that Powell grows in test plots are not allowed to flower. The only exceptions are the trees growing in plots on Maynard and Powell's research farm.

Some of these closely monitored transgenic trees are producing catkins. Any catkins that will not be used for pollen collection must be removed from the tree as soon as they appear. The catkins whose pollen will be collected for use in breeding are covered with special bags that prevent the pollen from escaping into the air.

When a bagged catkin reaches maturity, the scientists collect the pollen and use it to pollinate the female flowers of pure American chestnut trees. The baby trees will receive half of their genetic material from each parent. Because inheritance is a question of odds, it's likely that about half of the babies produced by this breeding will inherit the OxO genes and be blight resistant like their father. The other half won't inherit the gene from their father, and they can't get it from their mother (the pure American chestnut tree), which doesn't have it. Powell's team has another test that quickly determines whether a baby has the OxO genes. Only babies that inherit the OxO genes (the blight-resistance shield) are used for further breeding.

OxO genes are dominant genes. Eventually, some of the babies in future generations will receive OxO genes from their father *and* from their mother. When these babies mature and become parent trees, all their babies will be blight resistant.

FINAL APPROVAL

Before transgenic American chestnut trees can be freely planted in orchards, fields, and forests, scientists must show that they will not negatively affect the environment. They must show that the trees won't change the soil in a way that spoils the soil's composition. So far, the decomposition of transgenic chestnut leaves shows no sign of altering the soil in unexpected ways. Examination of the microbes and creatures that normally live in the soil around chestnut roots has shown no differences. Nor have any behavioral differences been observed in the insects that inhabit or visit the transgenic trees.

Scientists must also prove that the trees won't harm the food chain. The nuts must be safe for animals and people to eat. How—or even if—transgenic chestnut seeds (the nuts) differ nutritionally from other chestnuts is still being researched.

Obtaining approval from the USDA, the Environmental Protection Agency, and the Food and Drug Administration to plant transgenic American chestnut trees outside of test plots will take at least several years. The lengthy process ensures that transgenic trees meet all the regulations.

Even though approval has not yet been granted, scientists are thinking about the future. Lines of transgenic American chestnut trees are not genetically diverse. Remember, a clone's genes are identical to those of all the other clones made from the same embryo. To increase their trees' chances of survival, Powell's team must keep diversity in mind. They must outcross them, which means breeding them with American chestnut trees that have different genetic makeups. Doing this maintains and captures the genetic diversity of the wild American chestnut trees that are still growing in forests around the country.

The New York state chapter of TACF is helping with this aspect of the breeding program. They are planting "mother tree" orchards of wild-type American chestnut trees for future breeding with transgenic trees. And eventually, the scientists plan to outcross transgenic trees with American chestnut mothers from other regions. This will increase the trees' ability to live in a variety of climates and environments.

Maynard, Powell, and their colleagues have bright hopes for the future. It seems particularly appropriate that in 2012, they planted 10 transgenic trees at the New York Botanical Garden, not far from where the chestnut blight was first identified in 1904. "The smaller trees we planted didn't make it, but the larger trees are doing great," reported Powell. But because of regulations, these trees are not permitted to flower. And if one of the surviving trees becomes too big for the staff to remove all its flowers, it will be cut to ground level and allowed to grow new sprouts, as billions of American chestnut trees have for thousands of years.

While virus-weakened strains of the blight fungus are spreading in West Salem, Wisconsin, Michigan, and orchards in other states, and transgenic trees are awaiting testing and governmental approval, thousands of TACF's backcrossed American chestnut trees are already being restored in forests in the eastern United States.

CHAPTER EIGHT

RESTORATION

AMERICAN CHESTNUT TREES WON'T RETURN to forests by themselves. "The tree needs help," said Laura Georgi, who has bred many hundreds of trees at TACF's Virginia farms. "What motivates me is the prospect of repairing the damage done to this magnificent tree due to the actions of man." It seems only fair that humans—the species responsible for bringing the blight to American chestnut trees—should help restore them to North American forests.

Restoring four billion American chestnut trees is unlikely, at least in our lifetimes. However, large-scale restorations can happen. There's an old saying: "Where there's a will, there's a way." Enough people have had the will to rescue endangered animals, such as the American bison, the bald eagle, and the giant panda, that were on the brink of extinction. Scores of scientists and thousands of people who love trees believe that the American chestnut tree is also worth saving. "There's something about them. They're like the giant panda of the forest world. For some reason, people care about the American chestnut differently than they do about other trees. Maybe it's because they have become part of our country's collective memory. They are an icon," said Anita Baines, a scientist who works at the West Salem chestnut stand. Restoration is a gargantuan task, but many people of all ages willingly lend their time and muscles. Because of this, the American chestnut is poised for a comeback of epic proportions.

ON BARREN LANDS

For many years, no trees, shrubs, or animals have lived on some mountain lands in Kentucky, Ohio, Pennsylvania, Virginia, and West Virginia. These are sites where surface coal mining occurred. In order to get to the coal, construction vehicles bulldozed the plants and stripped away almost all the soil. In some places, this spoiled the whole mountaintop. The desolate land, having been abandoned after the mines closed, is un-inhabitable since little soil remains. But American chestnut trees are hardy—when they are not attacked by the blight. Give them a bit of soil and adequate sunlight, and they grow quickly. TACF's Restoration Chestnut 1.0 trees are part of the plans to give these barren lands a new lease on life. And they are ready to go.

There are many benefits to planting chestnut trees at working and abandoned mine sites. The trees' roots,

In celebration of Arbor Day, these middle school students plant restoration chestnut seedlings on a reclaimed mine site in Tennessee.

spreading wide and deep, hold the soil in place so rain can't wash it away. The trunks, leaves, and nuts attract wildlife. And the promise of a supply of tall, straight lumber—a long-term goal of restoration—interests the timber industry.

During the planting seasons of 2012 through 2014, volunteers planted more than 14,000 chestnut seedlings at 12 reclaimed mine sites. The young trees were an assortment of pure American, Chinese, and backcrossed Restoration Chestnut 1.0 trees from TACF's Meadowview farms in Virginia. Even though scientists already knew that the pure American trees will eventually die from the blight, the pure American and Chinese trees were planted so scientists could compare how various types of chestnuts grow in soils left bare by mining.

Most of the seedlings came from plots of land dedicated to growing only chestnut trees. At the abandoned mine sites, they were planted alongside oak, poplar, and maple seedlings. This is a real-life test to see if blight-resistant American chestnuts can hold their own when forced to compete with other species of trees for survival.

Scientists will monitor the young trees for several years to check their progress.

For ease in shipping, many of the young trees were transported to where they were planted with bare roots—that is, without soil surrounding their roots.

"We say that bare-root trees on mine sites sleep, creep, then leap. The first year, they're reestablishing their root systems, which were disturbed when they were lifted from the nursery, and they're getting established in their new environment. The second year is much the same, but they'll start to grow a little. During the third and fourth years, they have good root systems and start to grow rapidly aboveground," explained Michael French, a forester with TACF. So far, he sees good results: 90% to 95% of the seedlings look healthy.

The volunteers also planted Restoration Chestnut 1.0 seeds (nuts). Drenching spring rains in 2012 drowned the emerging sprouts and rotted most of the seeds. But in test plots, most of the Restoration seeds germinated well. Under normal weather conditions, the seeds planted on mine sites are expected to germinate with greater success.

Restoring American chestnut trees reminds us of their importance. It's a way of remembering and honoring the past. And so, it seems fitting that American chestnut trees are also being planted in one particular place in Pennsylvania. On September 11, 2001, four terrorists hijacked United Airlines Flight 93. Tragically, the plane crashed in a field near Shanksville, Pennsylvania. Forty innocent people died in the crash. The field, which is a reclaimed mine site, is now the Flight 93 National Memorial. In 2012, in memory of those who died, more than 500 volunteers planted over

In 2017, many volunteers planted chestnut trees at the Flight 93 National Memorial.

22,000 seedlings, 1,500 of which were Restoration Chestnut 1.0 trees. In the years since, TACF has increased the number of chestnut trees growing at the site to more than 3,400. In 2016, during the fifth consecutive year of planting on the site, each one of the more than 300 volunteers was given the opportunity to plant a chestnut seedling.

IN FORESTS

Forests still grew after American chestnut trees died. Gradually, other trees and shrubs filled in the ecological gap formerly occupied by the chestnut. Although the

American chestnut was once king of the forest, TACF's Restoration Chestnut 1.0 seedlings are very much the new kids on the block. Their survival depends on whether they can compete successfully for sunlight, water, and nutrients against the trees that have replaced their ancestors. But, as foresters are finding, the American chestnut quickly takes advantage of a fair opportunity when it is presented.

The U.S. Forest Service is one of many organizations that have established a partnership with TACF. Restoration Chestnut 1.0 seedlings started their journey back to national forests in 2009. But making them a part of the forest ecosystem wasn't easy. The baby trees needed help to get a toehold. Where dense vegetation—competitors for soil nutrients and sunlight—surrounded the planting site, foresters sprayed the area with herbicides. They also placed protective collars around the tender stems to shield them from browsing deer. If the trees survive, they will become part of the forests' ecosystem once again.

TACF has 16 chapters, which includes people from 20 states. Five hundred chestnut orchards supported by TACF chapters breed trees and produce seeds for

Volunteers have planted thousands of American chestnut trees in these orchards established by TACF's state chapters.

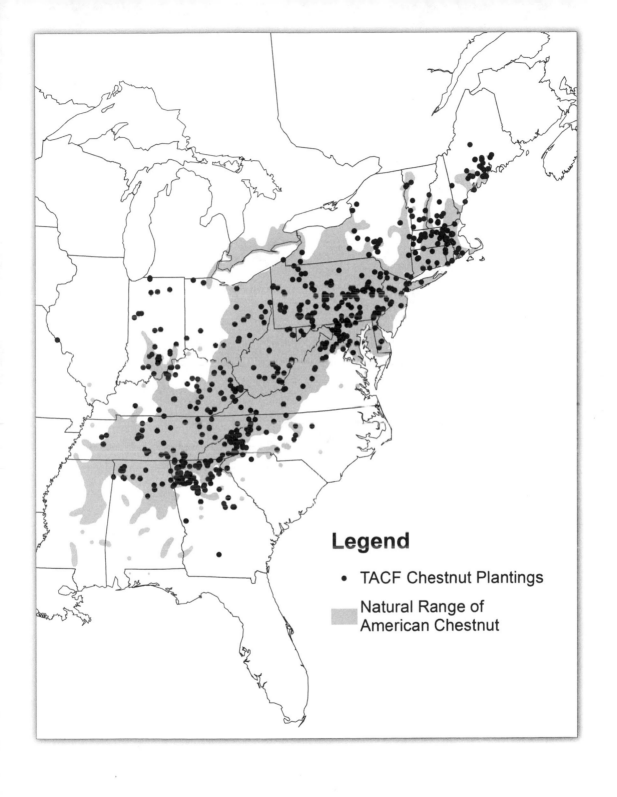

Legend

- TACF Chestnut Plantings

  Natural Range of
  American Chestnut

planting. They are crossbreeding pure American chestnut trees from their regions with Restoration Chestnut 1.0 trees from TACF's Virginia farms. The babies these trees produce are among those now being planted in forest test plots.

THE FUTURE

People who love American chestnut trees are cautiously optimistic that all three of the research approaches—backcross breeding, using weak strains of virus-infected fungus to combat lethal strains, and growing transgenic American chestnut trees—will work. But they also hope that their efforts will benefit other species. The comeback of the American chestnut could be a model for other large-scale restoration projects. "Humans continue to move pests and pathogens around the globe, precipitating disasters. Besides offering a hope of [American chestnut] restoration, our work also addresses the broader question of whether we can recover from other self-inflicted disasters of this magnitude, and if so, how. We have an approach that can work, and we are making progress. We can make a difference," said Laura Georgi of TACF.

Thousands of people have devoted millions of hours

to aiding the American chestnut tree. But they can't rest on their laurels yet. New dangers threaten the restoration's success. An insect called the Asian chestnut gall wasp, introduced in North America in 1974, makes its home inside American chestnut trees. There, it prevents normal shoot growth and flowering. Leaves, and sometimes the whole tree, die. Another disease, root rot, which is caused by a type of mold, is far more disturbing. It quickly destroys a tree's roots. After that, there is no hope of future sprouts—the only thing that prevented the American chestnut's extinction decades ago. Dealing with threats like these are ongoing projects that will need the help of future scientists—and lots of volunteers.

Restoration is a process that takes time and patience. But there's something about the American chestnut that entices people to become involved for the long term. As Anita Baines stated, "I've been working on the West Salem trees for 20 years, and I'll probably keep working on them until I drop dead."

When the American chestnut seedlings planted today mature, they will stand as reminders that hope and renewal—for people and for the natural world—are possible.

AUTHOR'S NOTE

WHEN I WAS A LITTLE GIRL, I often heard my father say, "You know you've got a good neighbor when he or she plants a tree." I was lucky: The neighborhood where I grew up—less than 12 miles from downtown Manhattan, New York—had lots of trees. The pin oak outside my bedroom window housed cardinals and blue jays; their clear whistles and raucous screeches woke me each morning. At night, the tree's leaves shushed me to sleep. The bark of the Norway maple planted by my parents when they first moved to the neighborhood taught me to be careful; if I wasn't, I would scrape my legs shinnying up its trunk.

One tree, a gigantic swamp white oak, was my favorite. It towered above the house two doors from mine. Cement had been used to patch a split in its trunk, and high above the ground steel cables supported its branches. At its base, a bronze plaque informed passersby that it was the oldest tree in East Orange, New Jersey. One day, using information from the plaque, my dad and I did some math: The oak had been a seedling in 1751—"my" tree was over 200 years old! From time to time, my father and I sat on our front stoop and discussed what the old oak might have seen during its lifetime. "George Washington was a teenager when it sprouted," my father said. "Lenape Indians may have passed by when it was young."

I was in high school when I discovered that my father had a favorite species of tree. In biology class, my teacher assigned a project: Every student was to collect and identify leaves from 40 trees native to New Jersey, glue them into a scrapbook, and write an essay about one of the trees. My teacher handed each student a copy of *Common Forest Trees of New Jersey* and told us we could use a leaf from any tree pictured in the book, except the American chestnut. "Finding an American chestnut leaf," he said, "is impossible. They are extinct, killed by a blight many years ago."

When I shared this information with my father, he told me that he loved American chestnut trees. "Every autumn," he said, "when I visited my grandparents in Pennsylvania, we collected chestnuts, then roasted and ate them. By then, most American chestnut trees *had* died from the blight. But that is not the end of their story, there's more." After hearing what my father said, I was determined to find an American chestnut leaf for my collection. My hunt was successful because my father knew the forests of northern New Jersey well.

He and I drove to a forest where he had seen chestnut sprouts years before. Less than an hour into our woodland hike, we spotted an American chestnut. Its trunk was only an inch in diameter and blight cankers marred its bark. But its leaves were still green. One of them became part of my leaf collection.

As I researched this book, I finally understood why my father admired the American chestnut, and I began to appreciate them, too. The American chestnut's story is of a tree that received what could have been a knockout punch. But, like a champion boxer, it didn't give up the fight. Neither have the many people who have spent countless hours, many of them as volunteers, in the effort to help American chestnut trees survive.

Sally Walker and European chestnut tree

A trunkful of thanks—pun intended—to the crew at TACF's Meadowview farms in Virginia. As part of the Road Scholar program, I inoculated many of the farms' trees with the blight fungus. Fred Hebard shared his expertise in tree care and the ins and outs of backcross breeding. Laura Georgi taught me how to inoculate the trees. TACF's American chestnut orchards are breathtaking. Surrounded by hundreds of trees in various stages of growth, I could only think how much my father would have loved it there. At first, when I realized that my efforts would cause many of the beautiful trees to die from the blight, I was horrified. But restoration of the American chestnut will only be successful if the most blight-resistant trees are planted. And the only way to identify them is to infect them with the blight and see what happens. And so, I got to work. The process of inoculating the trees made my knees ache and my back stiff; it gave me a new respect for agricultural workers. But the experience was worth it. By inoculating the trees, my new friends and I helped Hebard and Georgi identify which trees held the most hope for a blight-safe future.

Thanks also to TACF's Sara Fitzsimmons and Michael French for their updates on reforestation efforts.

William Powell, Chuck Maynard, Linda McGuigan, and Andy Newhouse generously gave their time to explain the processes used to produce transgenic trees. Caring for such fragile baby plants is tedious work, but the results offer a great deal of promise. It will be interesting to see future developments as the program continues its quest for American chestnut trees with the internal blight-fighter shield.

Sandra Anagnostakis and Dennis Fulbright shared

their experiences working with hypovirulent (virus-weakened) strains of the blight. I appreciate their patience in answering my many questions about a very complex topic. Also, thanks to Anita Baines at the University of Wisconsin, who graciously shared her knowledge of the West Salem, Wisconsin, trees and their response to hypovirulence.

Also, a special thanks to junior high science teacher Megan Newhouse and the members of The Chestnut Club: Gabrielle Kehoe, Sarah Potter, Alethea Banerjee, Sydney Smith, Adyson Burke, and Trinity Dearden. They read an early version of the manuscript and gave me wonderful feedback. And they feasted on roasted chestnuts while doing so!

Restoring American chestnuts to forests will impact animal populations. I found the seed preference study (see Appendix B) done by Robert Swihart and Rita Blythe absolutely fascinating, and they willingly shared their results with me.

It's important to involve young people in scientific research. The South Fork Conservancy, based in Atlanta, Georgia, is wonderful about reaching out to elementary school students. Thanks to the conservancy's Sally Sears for connecting me with Valerie Taylor and Thomas Rudolph (see Appendix C), who gladly explained their classroom science project. Let's hope that the trees they planted will grace the land for years to come. Also in Georgia, Martin Cipollini provided me with information about breeding restoration-quality trees and the dwindling bank of re-sprouting chestnuts.

I couldn't have written this book without the help of all these people and the hundreds more who work with them. Their efforts are making a dream become reality.

APPENDIX A

SCIENTIFIC CLASSIFICATION

The scientific classification system is like a set of nesting dolls—a set of progressively smaller dolls that fit inside the larger one. From largest to smallest, the scientific classification system contains seven levels from most general to most specific: kingdom, division (for plants and fungi) or phylum (for animals), class, order, family, genus, and species. Scientists classify living organisms into groups according to similarities such as shared characteristics and common ancestry. Each level describes more specific similarities the organisms must share to be classified in that particular group.

This is the scientific classification for American chestnut:

KINGDOM: Plantae

DIVISION: Magnoliophyta

CLASS: Magnoliopsida

ORDER: Fagales

FAMILY: Fagaceae

GENUS: *Castanea*

SPECIES: *Castanea dentata*

The genus and species in an organism's scientific name are always italicized; the genus is capitalized, but the species is lowercase.

These are the names of the other three species of chestnut discussed in this book:

Chinese chestnut—*Castanea mollissima*

European chestnut—*Castanea sativa*

Japanese chestnut—*Castanea crenata*

Since William Murrill first identified the blight fungus, scientists have reexamined it several times. This led to re-classification and new scientific names. The scientific name that is used today is *Cryphonectria parasitica*.

KINGDOM: Fungi

DIVISION: Ascomycota

CLASS: Sordariomycetes

ORDER: Diaporthales

FAMILY: Cryphonectriaceae

GENUS: *Cryphonectria*

SPECIES: *Cryphonectria parasitica*

APPENDIX B

A NUTTY SMORGASBORD

Scientists need to know how the wide-scale restoration of American chestnut trees in forests might affect animal behavior. Robert Swihart, a wildlife ecology professor at Purdue University, and his then graduate student Rita Blythe wondered if seed-eating rodents, such as squirrels, that were accustomed to eating acorns, hickory nuts, and black walnuts would eat chestnuts—a food they had never tasted.

Seed-eating animals and nut-producing trees benefit each other. The animals gather the nuts. They eat some of them, but they also carry some away and bury them for winter meals. However, they don't usually eat all their buried nuts. These unclaimed nuts germinate and grow. If rodents chose American chestnuts and buried them, it would naturally speed up the restoration process. Swihart and Blythe developed a test to learn what would happen when white-footed mice, eastern chipmunks, and three species of squirrels were offered a choice of different kinds of nuts.

The biologists identified stands of trees where the rodents lived. Then their team set up 30 seed stations. A seed station is a board with 81 small wells drilled into it. Each well held one nut. The scientists used nine kinds of seeds that included

Rita Blythe places several kinds of nuts into the cups on one of the feeding stations.

acorns, hickory nuts, black walnuts, pure American chestnuts, and backcross chestnuts. They offered both pure American chestnuts and backcross chestnuts to see if the rodents had a preference between the two.

Before placing the nuts on the seed station, Blythe drilled a hole in every nut. She attached a neon-colored tag to each nut with a strand of thin wire. The flag made the nut easy to spot after an animal removed it from a seed station. Once Blythe and her colleagues found it, they recorded how far the nut had been carried, whether it had been eaten, or if it had been buried.

Determining which nuts the different species of rodents chose was easy. "A motion-activated camera was mounted on the tree above [each feeding station], about five feet high," said Swihart. When an animal took a nut, the camera captured the choice with a series of photos.

Blythe uncovered the seed stations twice a day, shortly before the different rodents became active. She opened seed trays at sunrise for tree squirrels and chipmunks, who forage during the day. The trays for nighttime foragers, such as mice, were opened at sunset. Blythe covered these trays with chicken-wire cages to keep larger visitors, such as raccoons, away from the seeds.

At first, the rodents—squirrels, especially—weren't eager to visit seed stations. "Coaxing them to it was the hard part," Blythe recalled. But after tempting them with sunflower seeds, the animals became interested and continued to visit the stations even after the sunflower seeds were removed. The researchers conducted their study during several seasons from 2011 to 2014.

Overall, the researchers found that the mice, chipmunks, and flying squirrels chose both types of chestnuts over the hickory nuts, walnuts, and most acorns. Fox squirrels and eastern gray squirrels chose the other nuts, most of which were larger than the chestnuts. But what the squirrels did with the nuts after

A gray squirrel runs off with a walnut chosen from the feeding station.

they took them from the seed station was interesting. They ate more of the chestnuts and buried more of the other nuts. That means more oak, hickory, and black walnut seeds had the opportunity to germinate. One of the hopes for a widespread natural restoration of the American chestnut depends on seeds being carried away from the parent tree and buried in places where they can germinate.

A second interesting discovery was that all the rodents did take chestnuts from the seed stations, but all except fox squirrels preferred pure American chestnuts over the backcross chestnuts. This suggests that even though the trees are almost identical genetically, animals perceive a difference and may not treat the seeds in the same way. In that sense, the backcross trees may not be the ecological equivalents of pure American chestnuts.

What do the results of the nutty smorgasbord mean? This was one small study conducted in one region. Squirrels visited these seed stations primarily in the spring, a time of year when seed-gathering rodents are eating more food than they bury. Might the same animals make different choices during the autumn, as winter approaches? How would similar animal species in different regions respond? What if transgenic American chestnuts were available and offered? And if chestnut seeds were buried and the trees became widely dispersed, how would that affect the existing ecology of the forest?

"For now, we can say that the results with chestnuts were intriguing and unexpected, and the study raised as many questions as answers. But then, that's science!" Swihart exclaimed.

APPENDIX C

CHESTNUTS AT SCHOOL

Today, young people studying at all educational levels hold restoration success in their hands. They are the ones whose interest will carry the mission forward. Throughout the range of the American chestnut, they and their teachers are eagerly responding to the challenge. Many elementary, middle, and high schools have incorporated into their curricula the story of the American chestnut tree and the activity of planting seeds.

Fifth-grade teacher Valerie Taylor at Morningside Elementary School in Atlanta, Georgia, was intrigued when she learned about the plight of the American chestnut tree. And she saw a way for her students to have fun with science. The South Fork Conservancy, an Atlanta nonprofit organization that fosters connections between people and the environment, provided Taylor with an assortment of chestnuts: some were pure American, some were pure Chinese, and some were hybrids (crosses of the two species). The project Taylor had envisioned—growing chestnut seedlings—started in March 2014 and continued even after school was dismissed for the summer.

Like Taylor's other students, Thomas Rudolph didn't know anything about chestnut trees. That soon changed. "First Ms. Taylor gave us a lesson on trees and how to care for seeds. Then people from South Fork gave us a talk on why the American chestnut trees died. I thought it was very, very interesting, and I really liked the idea of planting trees in our classroom," explained Rudolph.

Rudolph and his classmates planted 37 nuts in black plastic cups. "It took about two weeks before we saw any signs that the seeds were growing. I was surprised at how fast they grew after that," said Rudolph. Only 30 seeds germinated. But, as his teacher added, "that was a good lesson in itself: Every science experiment doesn't turn out the way you hope."

Taylor's students monitored the seedlings' growth. "We kept a notebook and wrote information about the trees in it. More than once, we measured the stems to see how tall and how thick

These students who were in Ms. Taylor's class at Morningside Elementary School enjoyed being plant scientists.

they were. And we also measured the leaves' length and width. It was the best science project we did all year," Rudolph stated.

After the school year ended, the seedlings summered in the greenhouse of a local business. During that time, Rudolph helped to re-pot the seedlings, which by then were about a foot tall, into larger containers. Later, he helped other volunteers plant the seedlings on land maintained by the conservancy. In the process, Rudolph and his classmates learned more than just information about chestnut trees and science. They also learned that one person who plants a tree can make a difference.

UNDER A SPREADING CHESTNUT TREE

One of my favorite poems is "The Village Blacksmith," written about 1840 by the American poet Henry Wadsworth Longfellow. It begins: "Under a spreading chestnut tree / The village smithy stands."

The tree in this poem's first line was a real tree in the Cambridge, Massachusetts, neighborhood where Longfellow lived. It grew beside blacksmith Dexter Pratt's smithy. When the city widened the street nearby in 1876, the more than sixty-year-old tree was cut down. Eight hundred children who lived in Cambridge donated money for a special present that paid tribute to the tree and the poem. With the money they collected, the children hired cabinetmaker H. Edgar Hartwell to make a chair from the felled tree's wood. They presented the chair to Longfellow in 1879 for the poet's 72nd birthday.

I remembered the poem and the chair while I was working on this book. I thought: a famous chair made from an American chestnut tree—what a great connection for my book. But doubts crept in after I hunted down a photograph of the chair. When Hartwell made the chair, he carved leaves on it. Looking closely, I realized that they did not look like American chestnut leaves; the leaves carved on Longfellow's chair looked like *horse* chestnut leaves. The horse chestnut tree does not belong to the genus *Castanea*. The horse chestnut, whose scientific name is *Aesculus hippocastanum*, isn't even in the same scientific family as the American chestnut! What if Longfellow's tree wasn't an American chestnut, as so many people believe?

I wrote to David Daly, curator of the collections at the Longfellow House–Washington's Headquarters museum in Cambridge. He informed me that I wasn't the only person who had noticed the discrepancy in leaf appearance. Like me, others had also asked if the poem's spreading chestnut tree was an American chestnut. Visual examination of the chair's wood couldn't answer the question, so

The shape of the leaves carved on the chair provided the first clue that the tree mentioned in Longfellow's poem was not an American chestnut.

researchers turned to science. "[Scientific] analysis of the wood from the chair made from the 'spreading chestnut tree' indicates that it is not an American chestnut, but rather a horse chestnut or buckeye," Daly confirmed.

Then he told me something else: In 1880, children gave Longfellow another present, this time a book. "The book's front cover incorporates a piece of wood, originally from the tree, which has been carved into an image of children watching the blacksmith at work, with the horse-chestnut tree visible in the foreground." The book is in the collection at the Longfellow museum. While slightly disappointed that Longfellow's famous chestnut tree hadn't been an American chestnut, I was glad to find a new tree story.

"Under a spreading chestnut tree
The village smithy stands;"

Henry W. Longfellow sketched Dexter Pratt's blacksmith shop and the horse-chestnut tree that grew alongside it.

SOURCE NOTES

CHAPTER ONE: DISASTER!

12 "My observations . . . so great": William A. Murrill, "A New Chestnut Disease," *Torreya* 6, no. 9 (1906): 188.

12 "I believe . . . the fungus": W. A. Murrill, "Further Remarks on a Serious Chestnut Disease," *Journal of the New York Botanical Garden* 7, no. 81 (1906): 205–6.

14 By 1911 . . . Park remained: "Trees Soon Extinct," *Washington Post*, August 14, 1911.

14 Others resorted . . . nails or sulfur: "Trees Soon Extinct."

CHAPTER TWO: A FOREST GIANT

15 Chestnut trees . . . even longer: Ana Ronderos, "Where Giants Once Stood," *Journal of Forestry* 98, no. 2: 10.

17 "Where there . . . be chestnuts": William B. Rye, ed., *The Discovery and Conquest of Terra Florida, by Don Ferdinando de Soto and Six Hundred Spaniards His Followers . . .*, trans. Richard Hakluyt (London, 1851), 169, archive.org/stream/discoveryconques00ryewrich.

18 "inclosed with . . . of chestnut)": Thomas Jefferson to George Washington, June 18, 1792, Notes, *The Works of Thomas Jefferson*, Federal Edition, ed. Paul Leicester Ford (New York: G.P. Putnam's Sons, 1904), 7:117, memory.loc.gov/service/mss/mtj//mtj1/016/016_0731_0735.pdf.

19 In January 1876 . . . were interested: "The Treasure That Was Found in a Tree," *Reading Times and Dispatch* (Reading, PA), February 24, 1876.

21 In 1919 . . . 6 inches: "Enormous Chestnut Tree," *Durham Morning Herald* (Durham, NC), May 16, 1919.

21 Very large . . . people said: Donald Edward Davis, *Where There Are Mountains: An Environmental History of the Southern Appalachians* (Athens, GA: University of Georgia Press, 2000), 194, www.ulib.niu.edu:3701/lib /niluniv/docDetail.action?docID=10453775.

21 Georgia resident . . . and clothes: Eliot Wigginton, ed., *Foxfire 6* (Garden City, NY: Anchor Press/Doubleday, 1980), 403.

22 "more profitable . . . apple orchards": "Gathered About Town," *New York Times*, September 15, 1896.

22 In the late . . . chestnut trees: Susan Freinkel, *American Chestnut* (Berkeley, CA: University of California Press, 2007), 26.

23 As much as 34 . . . vanished: S.J. Diamond et al., "Hard Mast Production Before and After the Chestnut Blight," *Southern Journal of Applied Forestry* 24, no. 4 (2000): 196.

CHAPTER THREE: SEEKING THE SOURCE

27 In the late . . . United States: Sandra L. Anagnostakis, "An Historical Reference for Chestnut Introductions into North America," *Journal of the American Chestnut Foundation* 5, no. 1 (1990–1991): 31, ecosystems.psu. edu/research/chestnut/information/journal/vol5-issue1.

28 Frank Meyer . . . other gardeners: Isabel Shipley Cunningham, *Frank N. Meyer: Plant Hunter in Asia* (Ames, IA: Iowa State University Press, 1984), 10–12.

30 "There goes nothing . . . anything else": Frank Meyer to David Fairchild, April 1906, in Cunningham, 62.

30 Meyer collected . . . United States: David Fairchild, "The Discovery of the Chestnut Bark Disease in China," *Science* 38, no. 974 (1913): 297.

31 In 1899 . . . out of the question: Joseph R. Saucier, *American Chestnut . . . an American Wood* (Castanea dentata *(Marsh.) Borkh.*), Publication FS-230 (Washington, D.C.: United States Department of Agriculture Forest Service, 1973), 3–5.

33 The roots . . . buried roots: Laura Georgi, personal communication to author, June 27, 2014.

33 "The old stumps . . . found two": Martin Cipollini, personal communication to author, August 22, 2014.

CHAPTER FOUR: AN EYEBROW-RAISING DISCOVERY

37 Information about the blight fungus, oxalic acid, molecular bonds, and the effect of viruses on the various strains of the blight fungus is from Sandra Anagnostakis, personal communication to author, August 19, 2014.

43 As soon as . . . on their own: Sandra Anagnostakis, "Chestnut Research at the Connecticut Agricultural Experiment Station" (lecture, The American Chestnut Foundation 30th Annual Meeting, Herndon, VA, October 19, 2013).

CHAPTER FIVE: MIDWESTERN SURVIVORS

46 On a wintry . . . sent over time: Walter Sullivan, "Discovery of Blight May Aid Chestnuts," *New York Times*, April 20, 1977; Dennis W. Fulbright, "The Survival of American Chestnut Trees in Michigan," *Journal of the American Chestnut Foundation* 1, no. 2 (1986): 4.

47 "It's the only . . . of them healed: Dennis Fulbright, personal communication to author, August 4, 2014.

48 By the 1970s . . . 3,000 trees: Thomas J. Volk, "Tom Volk's Fungus of the Month for May 1998," *Tom Volk's Fungi*, botit.botany.wisc.edu/toms_fungi/may98.html.

50 One weak . . . Michigan virus: Anita Baines, personal communication to author, September 2, 2014.

CHAPTER SIX: IT'S IN THE GENES

55 "During our . . . a mission": Fred Hebard, personal communication to author, December 19, 2014.

56 But he was . . . captivated him: Albert H. Ellingboe, "Tributes to Charles Burnham and Angus McDonald," *Journal of the American Chestnut Foundation* 9, no. 2 (1995–1996): 4.

61 On April 15 . . . old to 90: Philip Rutter, "The President's Message," *Journal of the American Chestnut Foundation* 4, no. 1 (1989–1990): 1.

61 The next year . . . about 1,000 nuts: Frederick Hebard, "Meadowview Notes," *Journal of the American Chestnut Foundation* 5, no. 1 (1990–1991): 11.

63 By 2014 . . . 40,000 chestnut trees: Fred Hebard, personal communication to author, August 27, 2014.

65 A chestnut tree has . . . Chinese chestnut genes: William Powell, personal communication to author, September 3, 2014.

67 "Our near-term . . . on their own": Laura Georgi, personal communication to author, August 25, 2014.

71 In 2005 . . . restoration projects: Fred Hebard, personal communication to author, September 2, 2014.

CHAPTER SEVEN: HIGH-TECH ARMOR

75 But Maynard . . . each chestnut embryo: William Powell, personal communication to author, September 5, 2014.

76 Maynard and Powell's team . . . Asian chestnut genes: William Powell, personal communication to author, September 3, 2014.

78 "just when . . . shoot pops out": Linda McGuigan, personal communication to author, September 10, 2014.

83 While the leaf test . . . stem inoculations: Andrew Newhouse, personal communication to author, September 11, 2014.

86 To increase their . . . around the country: William Powell, personal communication to author, August 11, 2014.

87   "The smaller trees . . . are doing great": William Powell, personal communication to author, August 11, 2014.

CHAPTER EIGHT: RESTORATION

88   "The tree needs help . . . the actions of man": Laura Georgi, personal communication to author, December 8, 2014.

89   "There's something . . . an icon": Anita Baines, personal communication to author, September 2, 2014.

92   "We say that . . . grow rapidly aboveground": Michael French, personal communication to author, September 22, 2014.

92   Drenching spring rains . . . with greater success: Michael French, personal communication to author, September 22, 2014.

92   In 2012 . . . than 3,400: Lisa Sousa, "Planting Chestnuts at the Flight 93 National Memorial," *Chestnut* 29, no. 2 (2015): 9.

93   In 2016, during . . . a chestnut seedling: Michael French, "TACF's Mined Land Reforestation Efforts Continue in 2016," *Chestnut* 30, no. 3 (2016): 4.

96   "Humans continue to . . . make a difference": Laura Georgi, personal communication to author, December 8, 2014.

97   "I've been working . . . I drop dead": Anita Baines, personal communication to author, September 2, 2014.

APPENDIX B: A NUTTY SMORGASBORD

107   Then their team . . . between the two: Rita Blythe, personal communication to author, September 15, 2014.

108   "A motion-activated camera . . . five feet high": Robert Swihart, personal communication to author, September 11, 2014.

109   "Coaxing them . . . hard part": Rita Blythe, personal communication to author, September 11, 2014.

109   But after tempting . . . were removed: Paul Franklin, "Seed Selection and Small Mammals," *Journal of the American Chestnut Foundation* 27, no. 2 (2013): 16.

109   Overall, the researchers . . . pure American chestnuts: Rita M. Blythe et al., "Selection, Caching, and Consumption of Hardwood Seeds by Forest Rodents: Implications for Restoration of American Chestnut," *Restoration Ecology* 23, no. 4 (2015): 473–81.

110   "For now . . . that's science": Robert Swihart, personal communication to author, September 11, 2014.

APPENDIX C: CHESTNUTS AT SCHOOL

111   "First Ms. Taylor . . . in our classroom": Thomas Rudolph, personal communication to author, September 8, 2014.

112   "It took about . . . grew after that": Thomas Rudolph, personal communication to author, September 8, 2014.

112   "that was a good . . . you hope": Valerie Taylor, personal communication to author, September 4, 2014.

112   "We kept . . . did all year": Thomas Rudolph, personal communication to author, September 8, 2014.

APPENDIX D: UNDER A SPREADING CHESTNUT TREE

114   Eight hundred children . . . the tree and the poem: Personal column. *Wilmington Morning Star* (Wilmington, NC), March 10, 1880, page 3.

116   "[Scientific] analysis . . . or buckeye": David Daly, personal communication to author, January 14, 2013.

GLOSSARY

board foot—Cut timber is measured by volume. One board foot is a unit of volume. It is one square foot (12 inches by 12 inches) that is one inch thick.

CAES—Connecticut Agricultural Experiment Station.

canker—An area on a tree that is infected with disease.

catkin—The male flower produced by a chestnut tree.

colony—A group of organisms that live together.

crossbreed—To mate one species of chestnut with another.

deoxyribonucleic acid (DNA)—A molecule that contains the instructions that each cell needs to do its job.

embryo—A fertilized seed that can grow into a tree.

fungus—A living organism that does not have leaves or produce chlorophyll, the substance that gives green plants their color. Fungi are not plants, animals, or bacteria. In the scheme of scientific classification, they are in their own kingdom. To survive, fungi must live on plants, animals, or decaying materials.

gene—A unit of DNA or RNA that controls which of its parents' characteristics an offspring will have.

genetic diversity—All the different characteristics that individuals of a species might have.

herbicide—A substance that kills plants.

hormone—A substance that organisms make to affect their cells or organs.

hybrid—The offspring of plants or animals from two different species or genuses.

inherited—Passed from parents to their offspring through their genes.

inoculate—To introduce a substance into an organism to cause a particular disease or to stimulate the immune system to treat or prevent that disease in the future. When people are inoculated, it is with weakened or dead bacteria or viruses that allow the person's immune system to recognize them and be prepared to fight them off in the future.

outcross—To mate a plant or animal to an unrelated individual of the same species or breed. Outcrossing increases genetic diversity.

pathologist—A scientist who studies diseases and their causes and effects.

pollen—A powdery, usually yellow substance that consists of the male reproductive cells of a flower. It is used to fertilize a plant through pollination.

population—A group of organisms, such as trees, that live in the same place at the same time.

ribonucleic acid (RNA)—A molecule that is found in all living cells. Some viruses do not have DNA. Instead, RNA carries their genetic information. It helps a virus hijack the cells of another organism in a way that allows the virus to multiply in that organism.

spore—A reproductive cell produced by a fungus.

stand—A group of trees that are clustered together.

TACF—The American Chestnut Foundation.

transgenic—A plant or animal with DNA that has been changed so it contains genes from a different species.

USDA—United States Department of Agriculture.

virus—A nonliving microscopic agent that multiplies by infecting the cells of living organisms such as plants, animals, and fungi.

SELECT BIBLIOGRAPHY

BOOKS

Bolgiano, Chris, ed. *Mighty Giants: An American Chestnut Anthology*. Bennington, VT: Images from the Past, 2008.

Cunningham, Isabel Shipley. *Frank N. Meyer: Plant Hunter in Asia*. Ames, IA: Iowa State University Press, 1984.

Davis, Donald Edward. *Where There Are Mountains: An Environmental History of the Southern Appalachians*. Athens, GA: University of Georgia Press, 2000.

Freinkel, Susan. *American Chestnut*. Berkeley, CA: University of California Press, 2007.

Hamel, Paul B., and Mary U. Chiltoskey. *Cherokee Plants and Their Uses: A 400 Year History*. Sylva, NC: Herald Publishing, 1975.

Rye, William B., ed. *The Discovery and Conquest of Terra Florida, by Don Ferdinando de Soto and Six Hundred Spaniards His Followers. . . .* Translated by Richard Hakluyt. London, 1851. archive.org/stream/discoveryconques 00ryewrich.

Saucier, Joseph R. *American Chestnut . . . an American Wood (*Castanea dentata (Marsh.) Borkh.*)*. Publication FS-230. Washington, D.C.: United States Department of Agriculture Forest Service, 1973.

Wigginton, Eliot, ed. *Foxfire 6*. Garden City, NY: Anchor Press/Doubleday, 1980.

ARTICLES

Anagnostakis, Sandra L. "Chestnut Breeding in the United States for Disease and Insect Resistance." *Plant Disease* 96, no. 10 (2012): 1392–1403.

Blythe, Rita M., Nathanael I. Lichti, Timothy J. Smyser, and Robert K. Swihart. "Selection, Caching, and Consumption of Hardwood Seeds by Forest Rodents: Implications for Restoration of American Chestnut." *Restoration Ecology* 23, no. 4 (2015): 473–81.

Fairchild, David. "The Discovery of the Chestnut Bark Disease in China." *Science* 38, no. 974 (1913): 297–99.

Hoyle, Zoë. "Solutions from the Double Helix." *Compass*, no. 11 (June 2008): 6–9.

Jordan, Meghan. "The American Chestnut: A Legacy to Come." *Compass*, no. 11 (June 2008): 3–4.

MacDonald, William L., and Dennis W. Fulbright. "Biological Control of Chestnut Blight: Use and Limitations of Transmissible Hypovirulence." *Plant Disease* 75, no. 7 (1991): 656–61.

Merkel, Hermann W. "A Deadly Fungus on the American Chestnut." In *Tenth Annual Report of the New York Zoological Society*, 98–103. New York: New York Zoological Society, 1906.

Murrill, W. A. "A Serious Chestnut Disease." *Journal of the New York Botanical Garden* 7, no. 78 (1906): 143–53.

Murrill, William A. "A New Chestnut Disease." *Torreya* 6, no. 9 (1906): 186–89.

Payne, Claire. "Can Chestnuts Survive on Their Own?" *Compass*, no. 11 (June 2008): 18–20.

Powell, William. "The American Chestnut's Genetic Rebirth." *Scientific American* 310, no. 3 (March 2014): 68–73.

Shear, C. L., and Neil E. Stevens. "The Chestnut-Blight Parasite (*Endothia parasitica*) from China." *Science* 38, no. 974 (1913): 295–97.

Sullivan, Walter. "Respite from Chestnut Blight Seen." *The Dispatch* (Lexington, NC), April 25, 1977.

WEBSITES

For additional information about the chestnut blight fungus, see Columbia University's Introduced Species Project, www.columbia.edu/itc/cerc/danoff -burg/invasion_bio/inv_spp_summ/Cryphonectria_parasitica.htm.

For a time-lapse YouTube video that compares the growth of a virulent strain of the blight fungus with that of a hypovirulent strain, see "Apple test for virulence of C parasitica Powell," youtu.be/WOuRhsaQf08.

For a time-lapse video from the State University of New York's College of Environmental Science and Forestry that shows the responses of a pure American chestnut, a Chinese chestnut, and two lines of transgenic American chestnuts to inoculation with the blight fungus, see "Enhanced Blight Resistance in Transgenic American Chestnut," American Chestnut Research and Restoration Project, www.esf.edu/chestnut/resistance .htm.

The American Chestnut Foundation has a wealth of information on its website: www.acf.org.

IMAGE CREDITS

p. 3: The American Chestnut Foundation (TACF), Fitzgerald and Pinchot; p. 4, 10, 11, 27, 34, 37, 57, 58, 59 (bottom), 68, 70 (top), 71, 72: Sally M. Walker; p. 5: Forest History Society; p. 6, 7: Wildlife Conservation Society, reproduced by permission of the WCS Archives; p. 9: The LuEsther T. Mertz Library of the New York Botanical Garden [Archives]; p. 13: Special Collections Research Center, University of Chicago Library; p. 16: TACF, after Jacobs 2007; p. 17: *Gathering Chestnuts*, painting by Ernest Smith, from the Collections of the Rochester Museum & Science Center, Rochester, NY; p. 18: Great Smoky Mountains National Park Archives; p. 20: *Gathering Chestnuts*, "Scenes in Fairmount Park," *The Art Journal* (1875-1887), 4 (1878): 2, Brooklyn Museum Libraries; p. 23: Library of Congress; p. 24-25: Courtesy of National Park Service, Shenandoah National Park, F.W. Brueckmann; p. 28: Photographer unknown, "Portrait of Frank N. Meyer, "Special Collections, USDA National Agricultural Library, accessed June 1, 2017, https://www.nal.usda.gov/exhibits/speccoll/items/show/536; p. 29: Special Collections, USDA National Agricultural Library; p. 32: U.S. Forest Service, Eastern Region photograph courtesy of the Forest History Society; p. 38: The Connecticut Agricultural Experiment Station (CAES), Pamela Sletten; p. 42, 44-45: CAES; p. 49, 51, 53: Mark L. Double, West Virginia University; p. 52: TACF, Mark L. Double; p. 59 (top): TACF, Kendra Gurney; p. 62 (top), 95: TACF, Sara Fitzsimmons; p. 62 (bottom), 64, 70 (bottom right), 73: TACF; p. 70 (bottom left): Julia Tye; p. 76, 78, 79, 80: Linda Polin-McGuigan; p. 82: Andrew Newhouse; p. 90: Christopher Miller, Reclamation Specialist, Office of Surface Mining Reclamation and Enforcement; p. 93: TACF, Michael French; p. 101: James A. Walker; p. 108; Kyle Leffel, courtesy of Rita Blythe; p. 109: Courtesy of Rita Blythe and Purdue University; p. 112: Sally Sears, South Fork Conservancy, Atlanta, Georgia; p. 115: National Park Service, Longfellow House—Washington's Headquarters National Historic Site: LONG 4469, Ross Chapple; p. 116: National Park Service, Longfellow House—Washington's Headquarters National Historic Site. Color insert: Sally M. Walker, except where noted.

INDEX